GERMANY'S
COLONIAL DEMANDS

GERMANY'S COLONIAL DEMANDS

*Edited from the reports of the
Oxford University British Commonwealth Group*

by

A. L. C. BULLOCK

With a concluding chapter by

VINCENT HARLOW
M.A., D.Litt.
Rhodes Professor of Imperial History
in the University of London

GREENWOOD PRESS, PUBLISHERS
WESTPORT, CONNECTICUT

Library of Congress Cataloging in Publication Data

Oxford University British Commonwealth Group.
   Germany's colonial demands.

   Reprint of the 1939 ed. published by Oxford
University Press, London.
   Includes index.
   1. Germany--Colonies. 2. European War, 1914-
1918--Territorial questions. 3. Mandates.
4. Africa--Politics and government. 5. Versailles,
Treaty of, June 28, 1919 (Germany) I. Bullock,
Alan Louis Charles. II. Title.
JV2027.O9 1975   940.53'14   75-8482
ISBN 0-8371-8154-2

Originally published in 1939 by Oxford University Press, London

This reprint has been authorized by the Clarendon Press Oxford

Reprinted in 1975 by Greenwood Press,
a division of Williamhouse-Regency Inc.

Library of Congress Catalog Card Number 75-8482

ISBN 0-8371-8154-2

Printed in the United States of America

FOREWORD

THE Oxford University British Commonwealth Group was formed in 1935, with the object of studying and exchanging views upon questions of common concern to the member-units of the British Commonwealth. It is limited in number and is composed chiefly of undergraduate members of the University, with a few senior members. It is so constituted as to contain a quota of representatives of the United Kingdom, each of the Dominions, India, and some of the Colonies. Its object is to investigate selected problems in as objective a manner as possible, and although many different shades of political opinions are represented among its members, its discussions have avoided controversial clashes or 'tendencious' tone; at the same time, opposing views have always been expressed with candour, with tolerance, and, it is hoped, with common benefit. The Group arose from a conviction that there was great need for the different members of the Commonwealth to understand each other's peculiar problems and points of view, for it was believed—and experience has justified the belief—that only by such interchange could some measure of unity be found in the extraordinary diversity of the British Commonwealth. An 'imperialist' society, in any dogmatic or propagandist sense, the Group has never been, but has made its chief aim an impartial and fact-finding approach to questions which affect, in some degree or other, all parts of the Empire.

The method adopted is to work systematically through a programme extending over one or two terms and comprising different aspects of a general subject. At periodical meetings, sub-Groups, consisting of three or four members, read reports on allotted sections of the programme, and a general discussion follows. Professor Vincent Harlow has acted as Director of Studies since the inception of the Group, and under his guidance the following topics have been treated from time to time: Imperial Defence, the Machinery of Consultation among Members of the Commonwealth, Anglo-American Relations, the Ottawa Agreements, the Collective System in relation to the Commonwealth, Political Parties and Tendencies in the Dominions, the West Indies, and the question of the ex-German Colonies.

The present volume represents the substance of two schemes of study which the Group devoted, in 1937 and 1938, to the Colonial Problem, as it has now commonly come to be called. By that term, and by the title of this volume, we mean the specific demand for the return of lost colonies, rather than Germany's general colonial claims and policy, though these wider considerations are naturally touched on at many points. The second part of the book, which deals with separate areas, does not claim to be exhaustive; it

Foreword

seemed best to confine ourselves to the African Continent and to those more important colonies which have been most under discussion. On another page appear the names of those members of the Group who specially contributed to the investigation, either by written reports, by discussion, or by assistance in preparing the book for the press.

The composite work of many different hands inevitably suffers from defects which no amount of revision can wholly eradicate. Differences of style, of approach, and even of fundamental point of view are certain to occur, and cannot be completely reconciled. Every effort has been made to eliminate repetitions and overlappings, and to lend this compilation as much homogeneity as accords with an accurate representation of the different contributions: and where contradictory views have emerged, it has been thought best to call attention to them without attempting to reconcile them. These divergences, however, were not serious, and an almost complete measure of unanimity was reached in the general conclusions here advanced. For any 'sutures' which may still be visible to his offended eye, we would ask the reader to exercise such indulgence as may be consistent with just criticism. The work of revision and editorship, made the more arduous by narrow limits of time, has fallen mainly upon Mr. A. L. C. Bullock, to whom the Group stands deeply indebted for his indefatigable services.

Our thanks are due to the Royal Institute of

International Affairs for permission to use the Table on Raw Materials (reproduced from *Raw Materials and Colonies*) which appears herein as Table I.

Our indebtedness to other publications of the Royal Institute of International Affairs, and especially to *The Colonial Problem*, will be apparent from many references in the text.

It is unhappily necessary to add that while these pages were in the press, events occurred in Europe the effect of which on the considerations here presented it is, at the time of publication, impossible to estimate.

CARLETON KEMP ALLEN

RHODES HOUSE
OXFORD
10 April 1939

CONTENTS

Foreword by Dr. C. K. Allen		v
List of Maps		xi
List of Tables		xi

PART I

I. Introductory		1
II. The Peace Settlement and the Mandates System		11
III. Economic Arguments		47
IV. Political Arguments		84

PART II

V. South West Africa		118
VI. Tanganyika		144
VII. The Cameroons		168
VIII. Conclusion, by Professor Vincent Harlow		196

APPENDIXES

I. New Guinea, West Samoa, and Nauru		215
II. Mandates Constitutions		228
III. Trade of the Mandated Territories to-day and in 1913		233
IV. Population of Mandated Territories to-day and in 1913		239
V. The Congo Basin Treaty		241
VI. Allied Note of 16 June 1919		246
Index		271
List of Members of the Group		273

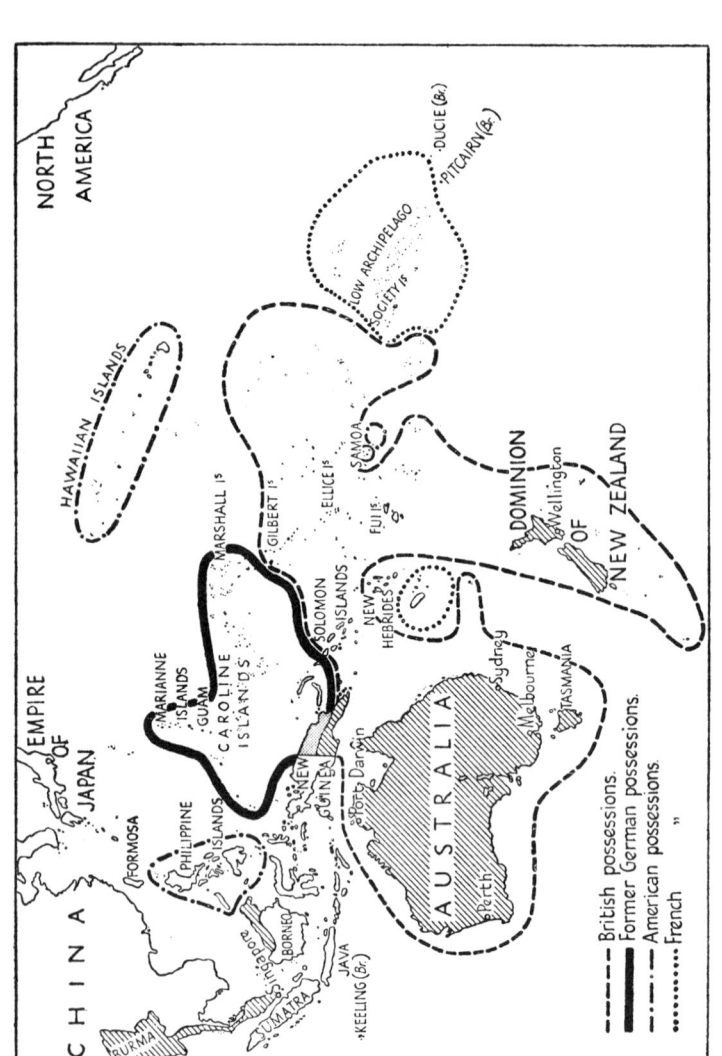

THE PACIFIC OCEAN
showing the former German Colonies

MAPS

Map of the Pacific Ocean, showing colonial possessions and
the former German colonies. *page x*

Map of Africa, showing colonial possessions and the former
German colonies. *page xii*

General Map of the World, showing colonial possessions and
the principal trade routes. *Back end paper*

TABLES

I. Showing the deficiencies in raw materials of the principal
states. *page 267*

II. Showing world production of raw materials. } *between*
III. Showing colonial production of raw materials. } *pp. 270–1*

IV. Showing proportion of trade with colonies in total trade
of metropolitan countries. *page 268*

V. Showing trade of colonies with metropolitan countries.
page 269

VI. Showing density of population in principal European
countries. *page 270*

AFRICA
showing British, Italian, and the former German Colonies

PART I

I

INTRODUCTORY

THE great period of imperialist activity in the nineteenth century came in the last thirty years before 1900. The period between the Franco-Prussian War and the beginning of the Great War is indeed one of the most intensive in the development of the great colonial empires. Many of the European states were concerned in the 'scramble for Africa'—France, Great Britain, Belgium, Portugal, Italy, and Germany—and it was in this period that Germany, the last of the great Powers to enter the colonial field, first acquired overseas territories.

This delay was due, not to any inherent incapacity of the Germans—on the contrary, they had always proved good colonists—but to her internal weakness, poverty, and division. Only in the last thirty years of the nineteenth century could Germany, united at last, directed by the genius of Bismarck, and equipped with the wealth derived from her industrial revolution, put forth her real strength in the world. The fact, however, that Germany was so late in entering the colonial field is of considerable importance. It meant, first, that the territories she acquired were not among the best, since these had already been secured by the other Powers; secondly, it meant that she had to stake out her claims in the face of an irritated

Introductory

opposition from other countries who looked upon her as an interloper. In fact, this period 1870–1914 is a troubled one in the history of Europe; the colonial rivalries contributed not a little to endow it with this character.

By the end of the nineteenth century Germany had acquired a considerable colonial empire with a total area of 1,053,000 sq. miles, a native population of 13,850,000, and a white population of 29,000. Where were these territories and what was their character? Since we shall be continually referring to the German colonies it will be as well to answer these questions at the outset.

Of the two groups of territories which belonged to Germany the African was by far the more important. It consisted of four colonies: German East Africa (now known as Tanganyika), German South West Africa, Kamerun (now known as the Cameroons), and Togoland.

1. *Tanganyika*, the largest of the German colonies, with an area of 393,500 sq. miles and a native population of 7,646,000, lies on the east coast of Africa, south of the Equator. It is bounded on the north by Kenya and Uganda, on the west by the Belgian Congo, on the south by Northern Rhodesia, Nyasaland, and Portuguese Mozambique, lying right athwart the British Cape-Cairo line through eastern Africa. The coastal plain, 620 miles long, from 10 to 30 miles wide, is bordered on the west by the steep eastern edge of the great plateau of Central Africa, which stretches

Introductory

back to a distance of some 600 miles from the coast, before the Belgian Congo is reached. This plateau has a mean altitude of 3,000–4,000 feet, and in the north is the great peak of Kilimanjaro, the highest mountain in Africa (19,321 feet). The country is well watered; some of its streams flow into the Indian Ocean, others into the three vast lakes of Tanganyika, Victoria, and Nyasa which lie along its frontiers.

Altogether some seventy-five distinct negro tribes inhabit Tanganyika, the majority of them of primitive Bantu stock, mixed with more recent Bantu folk who have migrated from the south. Along the seaboard, besides Europeans, live considerable Arab and Indian communities, who carry on much of the trading. The native peoples live mainly by agriculture, though the development of the colony has always been retarded by bad communications. The Germans built only two railway lines, serving the interior from Tanga and Dar-es-Salaam, the two principal ports: the latter, when completed, was 773 miles long and reached to Kigoma on Lake Tanganyika.

The greater part of German East Africa is now the British mandated territory of Tanganyika, but a portion of it became the Belgian mandate of Ruanda-Urundi, lying to the north-west of Tanganyika. German occupation of the country followed upon a period of commercial penetration, in which the chief agents were Karl Peters and the German East Africa Company. The German Government finally took

Introductory

over the rights of the Company in 1890, when a definitive settlement of the German sphere was reached with Great Britain.

2. *South West Africa* is a country nearly as large as Tanganyika (320,000 sq. miles), with a much smaller native population—only 80,500 in 1914—but with the largest European population of all the German colonies—14,830 in 1914. On the south it is bordered by the Cape of Good Hope, on the east by Bechuanaland, on the north by Portuguese Angola. It is a vast, unfertile, and sparsely populated country, the greater part of it a continuation of the high plateau of South Africa, some 3,000–4,000 feet high. Between the plateau and the Atlantic is the Namib desert, of an average width of 60 miles, sloping down to the sea. On the plateau in the south semi-desert conditions prevail: north of Windhoek the country is covered with bush. On the east the territory touches the Kalahari Desert. The climate is hot and dry, the rainfall low, and the land, except in the north, more suited to pastoralism than to agriculture. In 1914 there were 1,222 miles of railway, connecting the principal ports Lüderitz and Swakopmund with the capital Windhoek, with an extension southwards to the Cape frontier.

South West Africa was the first of the German colonies, Bismarck having extended imperial protection to the commercial ventures of Lüderitz in the Angra Pequena region in 1883–4. In 1888 the German Government took over control from the South

Introductory

West Africa Company. Since the War it has been administered as a mandate by the Union of South Africa.

3. *Kamerun* is a smaller country than South West Africa (197,500 sq. miles) but with a far larger native population, 3,326,000 in 1914. It lies just south of the great bend in the western coast-line of Africa, being bounded on the north-west by Nigeria, on the north by Lake Chad, and on the south and east by French Equatorial Africa. Like the two other German colonies, Kamerun is largely a plateau country, ending on the north and north-west in rugged, broken mountain chains: at the western end rises the great, active volcano, Mount Cameroon (13,370 feet) with a base of 700–800 sq. miles. Immediately south of this mountain lies the 20-mile-wide estuary first named by its Portuguese discoverers Rio das Camerôes ('River of Prawns').

The country has a characteristically tropical climate, unsuitable for European settlement. Large areas are covered by primeval forest and tropical swamps, the accessible parts being suited to tropical agriculture. The native population are Bantu-speaking negroes in the south and centre, Sudan negroes (mainly Mohammedans) in the north. They are primitive peoples among whom witchcraft and even cannibalism long prevailed: polygamy is still almost universal.

Although the Cameroons estuary has always attracted traders, the Cameroons remained the least developed of the German colonies in Africa: in 1914 there were only 193 miles of railway, though considerable plantations had been made on the slopes of Mount Cameroon, with a port at Victoria.

In 1884 the Cameroons were brought under German protection by Dr. Gustav Nachtigal, five days before the British Consul proclaimed a British protectorate over the Nigerian coast. In the following year the boundaries of the two territories were defined and the Anglo-German dispute settled. Since the Great War the Cameroons have been administered under a mandate of the League, the major portion by France, the rest by Great Britain.

4. *Togoland.* In the same year Gustav Nachtigal had annexed the territory of Togo. This lay between the Gold Coast and Dahomey on what used to be known as the Slave Coast, and had an area of 34,600 sq. miles. The coastal strip, 32 miles long, is made difficult of access by a chain of lagoons, behind which stretches a plain for some 50 miles. The country is traversed by a range of mountains (2,000–3,000 feet) in a SW.–NE. direction: the greater part of the territory lies west and north of this chain and is a table-land, some 600–1,000 feet in altitude. The climate on the coast is hot, humid, and unhealthy, though it becomes drier in the north: in the south stretch wide forests of oil palms, rubber, and timber trees.

The native inhabitants in 1914 numbered a little over a million. They are of various stocks and some forty languages are spoken. In the coast lands the

Introductory

inhabitants are traders or agriculturalists, in the interior largely pastoralists. The German development of Togo was striking. They created a port—Lome—and built 203 miles of railways. After twenty years' work Togoland was self-supporting, the only German colony in Africa to attain that position. Since the War Togoland has been administered under a mandate, the larger part by France, the rest by Great Britain.

The other group of German colonies lay in the Pacific; they were of far less importance, as colonies, than the African territories, and little has been heard of any insistent demand for their return.

1. *New Guinea*,[1] together with the neighbouring Bismarck Archipelago, comprises an area of 90,000 sq. miles, with a native population estimated at 719,000. The whole of New Guinea, which has a total area of some 312,000 sq. miles, was never under German control. In the early nineteenth century the Dutch established rights over the western half of the island which were admitted both by Germany and Britain. There was a fierce dispute between Britain (chiefly at the instance of the Australian Government) and Germany for the possession of the eastern half. This came to a head in 1885, when an agreement was reached by which Germany secured control of the north-east part with the adjacent islands, the

[1] The German part of New Guinea was formerly known as Kaiser Wilhelm's Land.

south-east corner, later known as Papua, being left to the British.

Even to-day there are parts of the ex-German colony of which very little is known. It is a mountainous country—the Otto Mountains reach 13,700 feet—and thickly covered with forest. Communications are exceptionally difficult and to-day increasing use is being made of the aeroplane. Problems of administration are scarcely less difficult. The Papuans and Melanesians, who constitute the population, are primitive peoples with elaborate social organizations of their own. They live for the most part by horticulture, and on the coast by fishing. The Germans succeeded in establishing a number of plantations, but without marked success; the most important development in recent years has been the discovery of gold.

With New Guinea were included a great number of islands, known collectively as the Bismarck Archipelago, the more important of which are New Britain, New Ireland, the Admiralty Islands, and the northern Solomon Islands (Bougainville and Buka). The German part of New Guinea is now administered by Australia under a League mandate.

2. *Samoa*, an archipelago of fourteen islands in the South Pacific. In 1889 a protectorate was undertaken by Great Britain, Germany, and the United States. This unsatisfactory arrangement came to an end in 1899–1900, when Germany received all rights over Western Samoa, and the United States over Tutuila and the other eastern islands. The area of the German

territory was roughly 10,000 sq. miles with a native population of 35,000. The islands are of volcanic origin and very fertile; they are well watered and contain forests remarkable for the size and variety of their trees. The natives are pure Polynesians, of fine physique and considerable social development. Since the War Western Samoa has been administered, under mandate, by New Zealand.

3. *Nauru*, an island of only 5,936 acres in the Pacific, a little south of the Equator. It is important because of its rich phosphate deposits, which were discovered in 1900, twelve years after Nauru's annexation by Germany. Since the War Nauru has been administered jointly as a C mandate by Great Britain, Australia, and New Zealand.

4. *The Caroline, Pelew, Marianne, and Marshall Islands*, four archipelagos annexed by Germany between 1886 and 1899, all lying in the Pacific Ocean north of the Equator. Their total area in 1914 was 5,160 sq. miles and their native population 15,000. They are scattered over a vast area, are important principally for strategic reasons, and since the War have been administered as mandated territory by the Japanese.

5. *Kiao-Chow*. In 1898 Germany seized the port of Kiao-Chow on the Shantung peninsula in China. Kiao-Chow was used by Germany as a trading centre and naval base in the Far East. It resembled the British settlement of Hong Kong more than the ordinary type of colony. Since the War it has become once more an integral part of China.

Introductory

This very summary account of the former German overseas possessions will serve as an introduction to the controversy respecting their future control and administration. We propose now to describe the conditions of their cession by Germany in 1919, and to examine in turn the legal, economic, and political arguments for and against their return.

II

THE PEACE SETTLEMENT AND THE MANDATES SYSTEM

I

BY Article 11 of the famous Congo Treaty of 1885,[1] to which all the Colonial Powers with possessions in Africa were parties, it had been agreed that, in the event of a European war, the Powers should, by 'good offices', endeavour to place Africa under the rule of neutrality. Yet in fact, before the end of August 1914, fighting had already broken out in Africa and by the early months of 1915 all the German overseas territories, except South West Africa and German East Africa (now Tanganyika), had been occupied. In South West Africa, after a difficult campaign, the German forces surrendered to Botha and Smuts in July 1915; in German East Africa General von Lettow Vorbeck maintained a brilliant and dogged resistance until the Armistice, although by 1917 the major portion of the country had been conquered.

It is a charge frequently met with in German colonial literature that the Allies were responsible for the extension of the war to Africa and the Pacific colonies, and that they showed as little respect for treaty obligations as any other Power, when these conflicted with their interests. The facts, however, so far as they have ever been established, do not appear

[1] See Appendix V.

to bear this out. It was the Belgian Government who, by their notes of 7 August to France and England, attempted to preserve the neutrality of the conventional Congo Basin and the French and English Governments refused their acceptance of the Belgian Government's request only on the ground that fighting had already broken out. The German claim that they took the initiative in trying to preserve the neutrality of the African territories of the European Powers is not consistent with the facts. According to the statement of the Belgian Government (dispatched to Berlin on 21 October 1914, by way of the Spanish Government), while the Germans claimed to have requested United States intervention in the interests of neutrality on 22 August, in fact no such request was heard of by them until 25 September. No explanation has ever been given for this delay and the suspicion remains that the German Government, finding that the war in Africa was going against them, and that the great offensive on the Marne had failed to achieve its purpose, then for the first time became anxious for the enforcement of the neutrality convention, and, to give a better impression, ante-dated their Note.

The question of who began hostilities in Africa has been the subject of much controversy. According to the Belgian Government the initial attack was made by a German force at Lukuga on 22 August 1914,[1] which was rapidly followed by a series of raids designed

[1] *Belgian Grey Book, No. 1*, Despatch No. 76; *Belgian Grey Book, No. 2*, Despatch No. 58.

to cut the Uganda railway. On 14 August, however, Admiral King-Hall had bombarded and destroyed the German wireless station at Dar-es-Salaam, which, as the British claimed, had been engaged in the 'unneutral service' of assisting German commerce-raiders.

With regard to neutrality obligations, the major portion of the German overseas territories—South West Africa, Togoland, the northern part of Kamerun, as well as the Pacific possessions—were subject to no commitments. In the territories which were affected by the Congo Treaty no question of a breach of treaty obligations did in fact arise, since neutrality was expressly subject to an option vested in the Contracting Parties of proclaiming neutrality (see Art. 10 of the Berlin Act, App. V); and up to the time when the fighting in Africa began, Belgium was the only Government which had attempted to exercise this option. This consideration, of course, applies to Germany no less than to the Allies, and consequently the whole discussion of responsibility for the first acts of war in Africa is somewhat academic.

A larger and less definite issue is that of general aggressive intent in Africa. In that connexion it is to be remembered that the outbreak of the Beyers-de Wet rebellion in the Union of South Africa was, to say the least, not inopportune for the German authorities in South West Africa, with whom certain of the rebel leaders are known to have co-operated. Neutrality in Africa was not so attractive at that moment to the German High Command as it became when the hopes of a swift and decisive victory began to fade, and it was not till then that a belated appeal was made to the Congo Treaty.

II

The Germans have never ceased to maintain from 1919 until the present day that they were unfairly treated in the colonial settlement at Versailles. They argue that the Allied Powers failed to keep the promises which they made in the early stages of the peace negotiations. In order to decide how far the Germans are justified in this contention some attempt must be made to review the course of the negotiations and to arrive at an answer to the questions so frequently asked. To what promises did the Allies commit themselves in the preliminary negotiations? How far were the Fourteen Points accepted as the basis for the settlement that was to follow? How widely did the actual terms of peace, at least in relation to the German colonies, differ from those implied in the earlier negotiations and in the Fourteen Points?

In considering these questions, it is necessary in the first instance to recall the situation as it existed at the cessation of hostilities.

After the failure of the great German offensive in the spring of 1918, the military position of the Central Powers rapidly deteriorated. Their man-power was practically exhausted: they were suffering heavily under the blockade: there was discontent among the

The Peace Settlement and the Mandates System 15

workers and in the forces. In July came the Allies' counter-offensive which drove the German line farther and farther back: on 15 September the Austro-Hungarian Government published a proposal of peace and on 29 September Bulgaria, Germany's other ally in Europe, signed an Armistice. The same day a general agreement was reached by the German Government to request terms of peace from President Wilson. It is as well to make clear that in doing this the German Government merely bowed to the inevitable. Revolution ('the stab in the back') did not actually break out until 3 November; yet by 1 October Ludendorff and Hindenburg were demanding the immediate dispatch of the request for peace. (Lersner's telegram to Prince Max of Baden, 1 October 1918.) On 2 October at Berlin, Prince Max of Baden addressed to Ludendorff and Hindenburg the definite question: 'Is the Supreme Army Command aware that the opening of peace negotiations under the pressure of the military situation may lead to the loss of the German colonies and German territory, especially of Alsace-Lorraine and the purely Polish districts in the Eastern Provinces?' Even so, Hindenburg replied, they must insist upon the immediate dispatch of the request for peace.[1]

While undoubtedly the knowledge that there was grave discontent within the country influenced the German Government in its decision, the determining factor was the insistence of the Supreme Army Council

[1] Temperley, *History of the Peace Conference*, i, p. 123.

that Germany had reached the limit of her military effort. The German argument that, had they known what the terms of the peace were to be, they would have fought on, will not bear examination. Neither Ludendorff nor Hindenburg was given to underrating the prospects of success, yet both realized that they could do no more than stave off defeat for a few weeks; they could not hope to reverse the military decision. Hindenburg replied to Prince Max in the interview of 2 October:

'The enemy on its side are constantly bringing into the battle new and fresh reserves. The German Army still stands in a firm position and has successfully repelled two attacks. But the situation is growing worse daily and can force the Supreme Army Command to serious decisions. Under the circumstances it is enjoined to break off the battle in order to spare the German people and their Allies useless sacrifices. Every day of delay will cost thousands of brave soldiers their lives.'[1]

The basis of the peace negotiations which ensued was the substantial defeat of the German military effort.

The first stage in these negotiations was the exchange of notes between the German Government and President Wilson. In this stage President Wilson acted alone and the other Allied Powers were not consulted. His conduct of the negotiations was, however, so astute as to remove all cause for reproach. The two most important points are to be found in the first

[1] Temperley, *History of the Peace Conference*, i, p. 123.

The Peace Settlement and the Mandates System 17

German Note of 4 October, and in the memorandum of the Allied Powers of 5 November 1918, after the President had laid the negotiations before the other Allies. Taken together these two notes make it perfectly clear that on both sides the Fourteen Points were accepted as the basis for any future settlement and that the only reservations made by the other Allied Powers in accepting the President's proposals —namely, for the further discussion of the clauses dealing with freedom of the seas and reparations— left untouched Point 5, which prescribed the basis of the colonial settlement. In the Note of 4 October, the German 'Government accepts the programme set forth by the President of the U.S.A. in his message of January 8th to Congress (the Fourteen Points) and in his later pronouncements, especially his speech of the 27th September, as a basis for the peace negotiations'. The final reply of the Allies on 5 November accepted the same basis: 'Subject to the qualifications which follow[1] they declare their willingness to make peace with the Government of Germany on the terms of peace laid down in the President's Address to Congress of January 8th 1918 and the principles of settlement enunciated in his subsequent Addresses.'

The situation so far is tolerably clear. The next point is to consider what exactly President Wilson had laid down as the essentials of the colonial settlement in the speech of 8 January 1918 and in his subsequent

[1] These referred to the question of the freedom of the seas and reparations.

18 *The Peace Settlement and the Mandates System*

addresses. Point 5 of the President's famous Fourteen Points reads:

'A free, open-minded and absolutely impartial adjustment of all colonial claims based upon a strict observance of the principles that in determining all such questions of sovereignty the interests of the populations concerned must have equal weight with the equitable claims of the Government whose title is to be determined.'

This declaration, now accepted both by Germany and the Allies as an integral part of the settlement to be negotiated, can be supplemented by other passages from Wilson's speeches in 1918. Thus in the Address of 11 February he said:

'There shall be no annexations, no contributions, no punitive damages. Peoples are not to be handed about from one sovereignty to another by an international conference or an understanding between rivals and antagonists. National aspirations must be respected; peoples may now be dominated and governed only by their own consent. Self-determination is not a mere phrase. It is an imperative principle of action which statesmen will henceforth ignore at their peril.'

Later in the same speech he declared:

'The principles to be applied are these. . . . Second, that peoples and provinces are not to be bartered about from sovereignty to sovereignty as if they were mere chattels or pawns in a game, even the great game, now for ever discredited, of the Balance of Power; but that, Third, every territorial settlement involved in this war must be made in the interest and for the benefit of the populations concerned, and not as part of any mere adjustment or compromise of claims amongst rival states.'

The Peace Settlement and the Mandates System

To these extracts may be added yet another from a speech of 4 July 1918 in which he insisted upon

'the settlement of every question, whether of territory, of sovereignty, of economic arrangement, or of political relationship upon the basis of the free acceptance of that settlement by the people immediately concerned and not upon the basis of the material interest or advantage of any other nation or people which may desire a different settlement for the sake *of its own exterior* influence or mastery'.

From Point 5 and the extracts from his other speeches it is obvious that President Wilson intended that the territorial and colonial settlement should be one based upon the widest conceptions of international justice and the principle of self-determination, that it should be completely removed from any idea of revenge, military triumph, or a Carthaginian Peace. For such a settlement the President had the backing of public opinion in the U.S.A., and also of influential circles in Great Britain. An anti-jingo philosophy had been propagated during the War by the Labour Party, *The Round Table*, the Inter-Allied Labour Conference, and publicists like E. D. Morel and J. A. Hobson.

Perhaps even more important was the fact that Mr. Lloyd George had expressed similar views in his speech of 5 January 1918. Prepared after consultation with the Cabinet, the Labour leaders, representatives from overseas, and the most important parliamentary leaders outside the Cabinet, Grey and Asquith, this speech was accepted as an authoritative declaration of British war aims. In the course of it, dealing with the problem of German colonies, Mr. Lloyd George said that they would be 'held at the disposal of a conference whose decision must have primary regard to the wishes and interests of the native inhabitants'. The governing consideration should be to 'prevent their exploitation for the benefit of European capitalists or Governments'. Native chiefs and councils were 'competent to consult and speak for their tribes and members'. 'The general principle of national self-determination is therefore as applicable in their cases as in those of other occupied European territories.'[1]

On the basis of Wilson's pronouncements and Mr. Lloyd George's speech of 5 January, the Allied Powers were committed to a settlement on the basis of impartiality and justice expressed in such phrases as free scope for self-determination, national aspirations, and 'no annexation'. There were, however, other influences which played their part in shaping the policy of the Allies at the Peace Conference.

America had entered the War late, her losses had been relatively small, and the American attitude towards Germany was different from that of France and Great Britain, who had borne the brunt of the struggle. Especially was this true of the French attitude, conceived in a vastly different atmosphere, conditioned by circumstances the force of which America could scarcely comprehend. For Clemenceau, for Foch, for the majority of the French people the

[1] Temperley, op. cit., p. 191.

The Peace Settlement and the Mandates System

struggle of 1914–18 was set against the background of 1870–1; it was upon their soil that the greater part of the fighting had taken place; they had suffered the greatest losses of all. To the French people in 1918 the idealism of Wilson,[1] the noble sentiments of international justice and impartiality, appeared somewhat unreal. They cared for one thing supremely, security against the threat of German military power to their eastern frontier. The result was a tragic division of outlook between the Americans and the French, and to a lesser extent between the Americans and the British, a division which vitiated much of the work of the Peace Conference and which has persisted in post-War years. Clemenceau, it is true, accepted the Fourteen Points as the basis of negotiation, but he showed a marked lack of sympathy for Wilson's schemes and clearly intended that a much sharper interpretation should be placed upon them than Wilson had envisaged.

Moreover, during the actual war years a number of secret treaties had been concluded between the Allied Powers involving the transfer of German and Turkish territories in the event of an Allied victory. The more important of these treaties for the German colonies were:

1. The Franco-British Notes of 29 March, and 11 May 1916, upon the division of Togoland and Kamerun.

[1] 'We have no selfish ends to serve. We desire no conquest, no dominion. We seek no indemnities for ourselves, no material compensation for the sacrifices we shall freely make.' (Wilson's speech, 2 April 1917.)

2. The agreement between the Allies and Japan, March 1917, over Germany's Pacific possessions north of the Equator.
3. The clause in the Treaty of London, April 1915, which promised Italy compensation, if France and Britain extended their colonial possessions in Africa.

Mr. Winston Churchill[1] has defended these treaties on the grounds that they were necessary and justifiable for the purpose of holding together the Alliance in the years before America came in. In Mr. Churchill's view, 'they were in the main simply convulsive gestures of self-preservation'. That is undoubtedly true: they merely followed the traditional procedure of allies engaged in war. They were made long before Wilson's views were formulated and before similar views in this country had gained a wide acceptance. Inevitably, therefore, the agreements thus reached ran counter in certain material points to the provisions of the Fourteen Points. Here was a pre-existing obstacle to the satisfaction of what Lord Milner called 'the idealistic spirit in which immediately after the War a great number of people had approached the problem of world-settlement'.

There were yet other obstacles. As a part of the general propaganda campaign on the Allied side, German pre-War administration in the colonies was severely criticized and German colonial ambitions shown in an unfavourable light. The criticisms were

[1] Churchill, *The World Crisis: the Aftermath*, pp. 129–33.

far from being unjustified, but they contained exaggerations which are easy to discern after an interval of twenty years. Moreover, in the embittered atmosphere after a life-and-death struggle, criticism was unlikely to be always judicious or restrained. As a result, the Allied statesmen, even if they themselves had been free from prejudice, were under pressure from a strong public opinion which demanded the taking away of Germany's colonies in the interests both of world peace and of the colonial populations. The return of the German colonies to Germany was not, from any point of view, a practicable policy at the Peace Conference. According to Mr. Lloyd George, even Wilson accepted this fact; he quotes him as saying: 'All were agreed to oppose the restoration of the German colonies.'[1] From this reported remark and the official interpretation of Point 5 which was subsequently issued with Wilson's approval, it seems evident that he soon became convinced that the 'claims of the Government whose title is to be determined' were not, in fact, 'equitable' and thenceforward concentrated his attention upon seeing that the future disposition of the territories should be in accord with the welfare and consent of the population rather than the self-regarding interests of the victors. On this he came into collision with a strong party who favoured open annexation. The principal representatives of this view were the delegates of the three Dominions, Australia, New Zealand, and the Union of South

[1] Lloyd George, *The Truth about the Peace Treaties*, 1938, i, p. 514.

Africa, anxious to retain for their own countries the territories which each had won at considerable cost, and the possession of which they considered to be essential to their own security. Probably the Dominions had the tacit support of the majority of the other delegates: certainly the French agreed with them. Already, therefore, before the Peace Conference began, it was clear that Wilson's views would not meet with universal or easy acceptance, and that there existed a strong party openly in favour of colonial annexation, and impatient of any attempt at internationalization.

The position of the British Government in relation to the German colonies was difficult. They had an understanding with France about Togoland and Kamerun, they naturally sympathized with the Dominions' desire for security. On the other hand, in the debates in the Imperial War Cabinet,[1] it was realized that annexation of the German colonies by Great Britain might expose her to charges of territorial greed and react unfavourably upon the vast British colonial Empire. Sir Robert Borden spoke strongly about this danger. The general opinion was in favour of some such compromise as was eventually found in the Mandates system, Mr. Lloyd George and Lord Milner being anxious that the U.S.A. should be a party to any settlement, and even, if possible, one of the Mandatory Powers. At the Conference the influence of Great Britain was exerted to soften the demands

[1] Lloyd George, op. cit., i, pp. 114–31.

The Peace Settlement and the Mandates System

of the Dominions and to persuade them to accept the Mandates compromise.

III

When the Peace Conference finally met at Paris in January 1919, Wilson was insistent that the League of Nations should be set up before the colonial question was discussed. But before the Covenant could be drafted Mr. Lloyd George raised the colonial question in the Council of Ten on 23 January. Wilson was very much disturbed by this; he saw that an important principle was at stake, for he had hoped to place the territorial and colonial settlement in the hands of the League, and not of the principal Allied Powers. Mr. Lloyd George, however, had the support of the other Allies; he could plead the urgent need of an immediate settlement and in the end he got his own way, the colonial settlement being undertaken before the League Covenant had been drafted.

The colonial issue was thus fairly joined. The alternatives which faced the Conference at this time were theoretically four. The German colonies might be returned to Germany; they might be given independence; they might be brought under international control; they might be annexed by the victorious Powers. Practically, however, the first two were impossible. The undesirability of the first was recognized, as we have seen, by Wilson; in the commentary on the Fourteen Points, approved by Wilson and later published by Colonel House, Point 5 is interpreted to mean that the colonies would not be returned to Germany, but that whatever Power managed them must act as the trustee for the natives under the League of Nations.[1] It is important to remember this when we are told that the colonial settlement was made in violation of Wilson's principles. Independence was equally impracticable. The German colonies were as yet too undeveloped to stand alone and would simply have been exploited by the trader and the planter without the protection afforded by a responsible government.

The practical alternatives were only two, annexation or international control, and upon these the discussion hinged. The Dominions' annexationist arguments were supported by M. Simon, the French Minister for Colonies. He considered international control to be frankly impracticable and believed that by annexation, coupled with the maintenance of the 'Open Door', the purpose of Point 5 would be best achieved. To this President Wilson refused to listen. They must, he insisted, agree upon the principle of trusteeship and leave its application to the League of Nations.[2]

Evidently some compromise had to be found between the two alternatives and the compromise adopted was that of colonial mandates. Before the Peace Conference assembled General Smuts, in his book *The League of Nations, Practical Suggestions*, had outlined such a scheme.

[1] Churchill, op. cit., p. 107.
[2] Lloyd George, op. cit., i, p. 533.

The Peace Settlement and the Mandates System

'The only compromise I make' (i.e. with the principle of racial autonomy), he wrote, 'and make partly to conciliate the Great Powers and partly in view of the administrative inexperience of the League at the beginning, is the concession that, subject to the authority and control of the League, which I mean to be real and effective, suitable powers may be appointed to act as Mandatories of the League in the more backward peoples and areas. That compromise will, I hope, prove to be only a temporary expedient.'

Smuts's proposal was not altogether original. There were precedents for the idea of trusteeship and international agreement in the Congo Treaty of 1885 (revised and confirmed at Brussels in 1890), and in 1815 the Concert of Europe had deputed Great Britain to watch over the interests of the Ionian Islands, though no right of supervision had been reserved by the Concert. Smuts himself had been influenced by other thinkers, especially the members of the Round Table group.

Smuts, however, had never intended to apply mandates to the German colonies. He had concerned himself solely with the territories formerly belonging to Russia, Austria-Hungary, and Turkey. As for the German colonies, he wrote: 'They are inhabited by barbarians who not only cannot possibly govern themselves, but to whom it would be impracticable to apply any idea of self-determination in the European sense.' But the mandates proposal offered precisely such a compromise as the Conference was seeking, and it was therefore applied to the African and Pacific German

28 *The Peace Settlement and the Mandates System*

colonies, as well as to other territories in the Near East. With certain important alterations both sides to the dispute were at length persuaded to accept the scheme and it was embodied in the Covenant of the League as Article 22, the actual drafting of the Mandates constitutions being left to an allied commission presided over by Lord Milner. Before going on to consider these documents, one important point should be made. By Article 119 of the Treaty of Versailles Germany surrendered her colonial possessions, not to the League (as Wilson had wished), but to the Allied and Associated Powers. It was therefore by the Allied Supreme Council, and not by the League, that the distribution of Mandates was made, and the rights of supervision were delegated to the League. The allocation of the B and C Mandates was accomplished by May 1919, and of the A Mandates at the San Remo Conference of April 1920. The constitutions of the Mandates were, however, approved in each case by the League.

IV

Article 22 of the League Covenant, which is the basis of the mandatory system, reads thus:

'To those colonies and territories, which, as a consequence of the late war have ceased to be under the sovereignty of the states which formerly governed them and which are inhabited by peoples not yet able to stand by themselves under the strenuous conditions of the modern world, there should be applied the principle that the well-being and development of such peoples

The Peace Settlement and the Mandates System

form a sacred trust of civilization and that securities for the performance of this trust should be embodied in this Covenant.

'The best method of giving practical effect to this principle is that the tutelage of such peoples should be entrusted to advanced nations, who, by reason of their resources, their experience, or their geographical position can best undertake this responsibility, and are willing to accept it, and that this tutelage should be exercised by them as Mandatories on behalf of the League.

'The character of the Mandate must differ according to the stage of the development of the people, the geographical situation of the territory, its economic conditions and other similar circumstances.

'Certain communities formerly belonging to the Turkish Empire have reached a stage of development where their existence as independent nations can be provisionally recognized by a Mandatory until such time as they are able to stand alone. The wishes of these communities must be a principal consideration in the selection of the Mandatory.

'Other peoples, especially those of Central Africa, are at such a stage that the Mandatory must be responsible for the administration of the territory under conditions which will guarantee freedom of conscience and religion, subject only to the maintenance of public order and morals, the prohibition of abuses such as the slave trade, the arms traffic, and the liquor traffic, and the prevention of the establishment of fortifications or military and naval bases and of the military training of the natives for other than police purposes and the defence of territory, and will also secure equal opportunities for the trade and commerce of other members of the League.

'There are territories, such as South West Africa and

certain of the South Pacific Islands, which, owing to the sparseness of their population, or their small size, or their remoteness from the centres of civilization, or their geographical contiguity to the territory of the Mandatory, and other circumstances, can be best administered under the laws of the Mandatory as integral portions of its territory, subject to the safeguards above mentioned in the interests of the indigenous population.

'In every case of Mandate the Mandatory shall render to the Council an annual report in reference to the territory committed to its charge.

'The degree of authority, control or administration to be exercised by the Mandatory, shall, if not previously agreed upon by the Members of the League, be explicitly defined in each case by the Council.

'A permanent Commission shall be constituted to receive and examine the annual reports of the Mandatories and to advise the Council on all matters relating to the observance of the Mandates.'

The constitutions of the Mandates, which, together with Article 22, form the framework of the system, are printed in Appendix II. The system had been accepted as a compromise; its terms were therefore studiously vague and on certain points the different Mandate constitutions appear to run contrary to the intentions expressed in Article 22.

In the first place, contrary to Wilson's and Smuts's drafts, the League was not given control over the allocation of Mandates, which was left to the Allied Supreme Council. In fact, the majority of the Mandates were granted to Great Britain, France, and the Dominions. Secondly, the League was not given the

The Peace Settlement and the Mandates System

right of direct supervision over the administration. Though far from being negligible, its control is indirect, through the Permanent Mandates Commission, the annual reports of the Mandatory Powers, and the right of petition guaranteed to the mandated peoples.

More difficult to reconcile with the fundamental ideas behind the Mandates system are the grading of the Mandates (especially the creation of C Mandates) and the amendment on militarization accepted for the French Mandates. The Mandates were divided into three classes: A Mandates: Iraq (British), Palestine (British), and Syria (French); B Mandates: French Togoland, British Togoland, French Cameroons, British Cameroons, Tanganyika (British), and Ruanda-Urundi (Belgian); C Mandates: South West Africa (Union of South Africa), Samoa (New Zealand), New Guinea (Australia), the northern German Islands in the Pacific (Japan), and Nauru (Australia, New Zealand, and Great Britain). The A Mandates do not concern us here, but the C class, 'which can be best administered under the laws of the Mandatory as integral portions of its territory', is exempted from the obligation 'to secure equal opportunities for the trade and commerce of other members of the League'. This means that in South West Africa, New Guinea, Samoa, Nauru, and the Japanese Mandated Islands, the 'Open Door' is not maintained, and a virtual monopoly of trade is enjoyed by the Mandatory Power.

In the French Mandates of Togoland and the

Cameroons, directly contrary to Article 22 of the Covenant which prohibits the 'military training of the natives for other than police purposes and the defence of territory', it is added that 'troops thus raised may in the event of a general war be utilized to repel an attack or for defence of territory outside that subject to the mandate'. The mandated territories are thus placed on a level with the other French colonies in respect of the very vital right of the Government to recruit native troops. It is indeed difficult to reconcile this clause with the words of the Covenant.

On two material points—nationality and sovereignty—the official documents give no clear declaration. Article 127 of the Treaty of Versailles reads: 'The native inhabitants of the former German oversea possessions shall be entitled to the diplomatic protection of the Governments exercising authority over these territories.' So brief a definition was not satisfactory and the Permanent Mandates Commission in its last Session of October 1921 set up a sub-commission to deal with questions of nationality. As a result of their recommendations, the League Council in its 24th Session adopted four resolutions to cover the problem:

(1) the status of the native inhabitants of mandated territories is declared to be distinct from that of nationals of the Mandatory Power:

(2) native inhabitants of mandated territories are not automatically invested with the nationality of the Mandatory Power, but

(3) it is possible for individuals to undertake voluntary naturalisation:

The Peace Settlement and the Mandates System

(4) native inhabitants become 'administered' or 'protected' persons under the Mandatory Power.

Even this did not altogether settle the question, as we shall see in dealing with Nazi exploitation of what is called 'dual nationality' in South West Africa.

The problem of nationality naturally leads to the far wider and more fundamental problem of sovereignty. The question where sovereignty, in a mandated territory, resides may seem academic and remote. Yet in fact it at once becomes of extreme importance, when the transfer of these territories is discussed. No procedure for transfer, as opposed to the termination of Mandates, was considered in 1919–20, and in fact the question of who is the sovereign in a mandated territory was never explicitly raised, largely because of the political situation. The Mandates system was accepted as a convenient compromise which would allow that awkward issue to remain dormant. The issue still remains unsettled and perhaps incapable of settlement.

Discussion of the question of sovereignty from the legal point of view lies outside the scope of this book. It has sometimes been suggested that no satisfactory answer can be found to the question, because the question itself is meaningless in such a context. In the words of a report adopted by the Council of the League in 1927, 'this relationship is clearly a new one in international law and for this reason the use of some of the time-honoured terminology in the same way is perhaps sometimes inappropriate to the new conditions'. This view has much to commend it. We are concerned here, however, only with the practical issue—who is to make the decision if the question of transferring a Mandate to another power is ever raised? And to that question surely the only possible answer is that another compromise would have to be worked out, as in 1919. No one sovereign power could make such a decision, but several would have to be consulted. Mr. Stanley Baldwin (now Earl Baldwin) as Prime Minister gave the following opinion:

'There are no provisions, either in the Covenant, or in the Peace Treaties, or in the Mandates, relating to the transfer of a Mandate from one Power to another Power and no such transfer has ever been made. I am advised that before any such transfer could be effected, it would be necessary that the consent of the Mandatory Power and of the Power to whom the territory was to be transferred, and also the unanimous consent of the League Council, should be secured. I hope that what I have said will make it clear to hon. Members that the question of the transfer of a Mandate is one which, were it to be contemplated, would require the most careful consideration and which would be subjected to a procedure of a very elaborate nature.'[1]

The view taken by the Study Group which prepared the Chatham House publication on the Colonial Problem (Oxford University Press, 1937) was that

'in practice, in the case of transfer of Mandated territories, the consent of the United States as well as of the Principal Allied and Associated Powers would almost certainly have to be obtained. It is unlikely that either the United

[1] Speech of 27 April 1936, quoted in *Germany's Claim to Colonies*, p. 63.

States or the Council of the League would give their approval to any transfer unless the instrument of transfer included the terms of the Mandate imposing conditions for the welfare of the subject people and it is very unlikely that they would consent to any transfer of B Mandates which did not include also the retention of the Open Door.'[1]

Experience suggests that should such a transfer be politically desirable and in the general interest of the Great Powers, a way would be devised for its accomplishment; until that time arrives, however, the legal difficulties may well continue to be regarded as formidable.

V

After the debate of December 1920, when the respective rights of the League Council and the League Assembly to control the Mandates were discussed, it was agreed that responsibility should rest with the Council, though an opportunity of discussion was given to the League Assembly in the annual debate on the Secretary General's Report. The Mandatories' annual reports are considered by the Permanent Mandates Commission, a small body of ten members, together with a representative of the International Labour Office. The members of the Commission must not be in the service of any government, though many of them have had experience of colonial administration.[2] The majority of the members are drawn from the countries without Mandates.

[1] *The Colonial Problem*, p. 94.
[2] Both Lord Hailey and Lord Lugard have been members of the P.M.C.

The sessions of the Commission are devoted to examining the reports and questioning the representatives of the mandatory powers. To read the minutes of the Commission is to be impressed by the thorough and conscientious way in which they approach their task. The British representatives, for instance, in recent years have had to undergo severe cross-examination upon Palestine. At the same time the Commission lacks real power to enforce its decisions; it is too dependent upon the co-operation of the Mandatory Powers. The value of the right to petition the League, guaranteed to the native populations under mandates, is liable to be seriously impaired by the fact that such petitions must be transmitted through the Mandatory Power, which can add its own comments and explanations. There was unanimous opposition on the part of the Mandatories to the suggestion that the Commission should interview petitioners, and the proposal had to be dropped.

There has been much criticism of the effectiveness of League control. It has been said that the Permanent Mandates Commission is too weak to enforce its decisions and that in the League Council criticism is always liable to be suppressed for political reasons. Certainly the Mandates system does fall short of perfection, but certainly too it represents an advance upon previous arrangements. In an atmosphere of publicity, abuses are not easily ignored, criticism is made and listened to, Mandatory Governments cannot lull public opinion in their own countries into too easy an acquiescence. The more liberal and progressive sections of public opinion have suggested that the Mandates system needs strengthening, but they have never urged its abolition; on the contrary, its extension to other colonial territories has been frequently demanded. The conclusion therefore that the Mandates system, though imperfect and in the nature of a compromise, does represent some advance towards international control and the closer recognition of responsibilities appears to be substantially correct.

VI

Criticism of the Mandates system in itself is one thing; but criticism of the Mandates system in relation to the expectations raised at the Peace Settlement, especially by Wilson's Point 5, is another. The Germans at the time, and persistently since 1919, have maintained that the colonial settlement was unfair and that they were deceived by the Allies. To understand the force of their argument we must take account of two factors: the strength of German feeling about the colonies, before and during the War, when the idea of a German Mittel-Afrika became one of the most popular of war aims, and the seriousness with which the Germans took the Fourteen Points and the Allies' pledge to respect them.

General von Epp has given a clear statement of the German case:

'Germany only gave her assent to the preliminary treaty of peace officially entered into on November 5,

38 The Peace Settlement and the Mandates System

1918, because she believed that President Wilson's Fourteen Points would be maintained and that the note of the American State Secretary, Lansing, of November 5, 1918, would be the juridical foundation of peace negotiations. Wilson's fifth point provided for a free, open-minded, and absolutely impartial solution of all colonial aspirations. This was subsequently nullified by Article 119 of the Treaty of Versailles, for Germany was forced to renounce all her rights to her overseas possessions. It is, moreover, impossible to justify the contention that the taking over of the German colonies was a veiled form of annexation to which the country must submit as one of the consequences of having lost the war, for the actual value of these colonies was not taken into consideration when the amount of reparations was fixed.'[1]

The same critical view was adopted by Mr. Robert Lansing, U.S. Secretary of State in 1918 and one of the American delegation to the Paris Peace Conference. After the Conference Mr. Lansing wrote:

'Thus under the mandates system Germany lost her territorial assets which might have greatly reduced her financial debt to the Allies, while the latter obtained the German colonial possessions without the loss of any of their claims for indemnity. In actual operation the apparent altruism of the mandates system worked in favour of the selfish and material interests of the Powers which accepted the mandates. . . . It seemed obvious from the very first that the Powers which under the old practice would have obtained sovereignty over certain conquered territories would not be denied mandates over these territories. The League might reserve in the mandates a right of supervision of administration and even

[1] Quoted in *Germany's Claim to Colonies*, p. 31.

The Peace Settlement and the Mandates System

of revocation of authority, but that right would be nominal and of little, if any, real value, provided that the mandatory was one of the Great Powers, as undoubtedly it would be.'

What did Germany want in 1919? The answer to that question may be taken from the German delegation's comments on the Conditions of Peace, forwarded to the Allies on 29 May 1919, in which Dr. Bell, Minister for Colonies, set out the German counter-proposals:

'Article 119 of the draft demands that Germany shall renounce all her rights and titles over her oversea possessions. This regulation is in irreconcilable contradiction to Point 5 of the Address to Congress of January 8, 1918, in which President Wilson promises a free, sincere, and absolutely impartial settlement of all colonial claims. The basis of every impartial settlement is that, before the decision, the parties should be heard and their claims examined. Article 119 at once rejects the German claims, without even giving Germany a chance to put them forward.

'Germany's claim to colonies is, first of all, based on the fact that she has acquired them lawfully and has developed them by means of incessant and fruitful toil and at the cost of many sacrifices. Her ownership of them has been acknowledged by all the Powers. Whenever conflicts have arisen with other Powers over particular sections of territory, they have been settled by means of agreements or arbitration.

'The possession of her colonies will be even more necessary for Germany in the future than in the past, since, if only on account of her low rate of exchange, she must be able to acquire from her own colonies, as far as possible, the raw materials necessary to her economic life. Her earning capacity having been reduced owing to the result of the war, she also requires the profits accruing from home production.

'Moreover, Germany needs her colonies as a market for her industries, in order that she may be able to pay for raw materials with her own manufactures and may have a field of activity for commerce. Germany is looking towards these resources to meet the liabilities imposed upon her in the peace treaty.

'Finally, Germany requires colonies in order to have territory where at least a part of her surplus population may settle, the more so as the result of the war increases the necessity for, and reduces the possibility of emigration.

'As a great civilised nation the German people have the right and the duty to co-operate in the joint task which devolves upon civilised mankind of exploring the world scientifically and of educating the backward races. In this direction she has achieved great things in her colonies. . . .'[1]

Two practical proposals were made: that the colonial settlement should be undertaken by a special commission before which Germany might state her case—thus would be achieved the 'absolutely impartial adjustment' of Point 5—and that Germany should be allowed to administer her colonies 'according to the principles of the League, possibly as the mandates of the latter, if a League is formed which she can enter at once as a member state, enjoying equal privileges with other members'.

[1] Quoted in *Germany's Claim to Colonies*, pp. 19–20.

The Peace Settlement and the Mandates System 41

The Allies did not accept these arguments. They were unanimous in declaring that the colonies could not be returned to Germany. Mr. Lloyd George[1] and Mr. Amery[2] have told us that this attitude was based upon strategical and political reasons. Mindful of the scheme, so popular in Germany during the War, for a German Mittel-Afrika, they refused to leave in the hands of their recent opponent the territories upon which this ambitious structure was to have been built up. After a long and bitter war with Germany—a war, moreover, in which they had been successful—the Allies had no intention of leaving Germany in possession of any territory from which she might once again threaten their security and peace. The entire world had been shaken by a war which they believed was due to unprovoked aggression, and they could hardly be expected to risk the recurrence of a spirit of militarism which they hoped had been permanently subdued.

These were the considerations which decided the policy of the Allies. The Allied Note of 16 June 1919[3] replied to the German counter-proposals as follows:

'The Allied and Associated Powers', so the note ran, 'are satisfied that the native inhabitants of the German colonies are strongly opposed to being brought under Germany's sway, and the record of German rule, the traditions of the German Government, and the use to which these colonies were put as bases from which to

[1] Mr. Lloyd George, *The Truth about the Peace Treaties*, i, pp. 114–31.
[2] Mr. Amery, quoted in *Germany's Claim to Colonies*, p. 56.
[3] See Appendix VI.

prey upon the commerce of the world, make it impossible for the Allied and Associated Powers to return them to Germany or to entrust to her the responsibility for the training and education of the inhabitants. . . .

'Germany's dereliction in the sphere of colonial civilisation has been revealed too completely to admit of the Allied and Associated Powers consenting to make a second experiment and of their assuming the responsibility of again abandoning thirteen or fourteen millions of natives to a fate from which the war has delivered them.

'Moreover, the Allied and Associated Powers felt themselves compelled to safeguard their own security and the peace of the world against a military imperialism which sought to establish bases whence it could pursue a policy of interference and intimidation against the other Powers.

'The Allied and Associated Powers considered that the loss of her colonies would not hinder Germany's normal economic development.

'The trade of the German colonies has never represented more than a very small fraction of Germany's total trade; in 1913 one-half of one per cent. of her imports and one-half of one per cent. of her exports. Of the total volume imported by Germany of such products as cotton, cocoa, rubber, palm kernels, tobacco, and copra, only three per cent. came from her colonies. It is obvious that the financial, commercial and industrial rehabilitation of Germany must depend on other factors.

'For climatic reasons and other natural causes, the German colonies are incapable of accommodating more than a very small proportion of the excess German emigration. The small number of colonists resident there before the War is conclusive evidence in this respect. . . .'

This Note has been very severely criticized as in-

The Peace Settlement and the Mandates System 43

sincere;[1] representatives of more than one school of thought have condemned it as a mere piece of sophistry designed to camouflage the true motive of territorial aggrandizement. Thus Mr. Harold Nicolson, while believing that the Allies did the right thing, holds strongly that they gave the wrong reasons. He dismisses the substance of the German case in the following words:

'I do not see that this [the German] argument has any validity either in law or in reason. Legally, President Wilson's fifth point is superseded by Article 119 of the Treaty of Versailles under which Germany surrendered her overseas possessions unconditionally. In reason, transferences of territory have always followed upon a successful war and to that extent Germany has no more "right" to her former colonies than Hanover has a "right" to her independence or Denmark a "right" to the duchies.'

But Mr. Nicolson continues:

'Yet although we may be satisfied that the legal argument is not valid either in law or in fact, we must admit that the circumstances and the spirit in which the colonies were acquired were not morally defensible. Had we frankly annexed these territories by right of conquest, we should be in a far stronger position to-day. The fact that we desired to seize the colonies and at the same time to pay lip-service to the Fourteen Points led us into one of the most flagrant acts of hypocrisy that even the Peace Conference committed and culminated in that appalling piece of jesuitical exegesis by which we explained that we could not give a Mandate to Germany owing to her maladministration of her colonies in the past. Instead of basing our rights upon military victory (which was a fact)

[1] For longer quotations from the Note, see Appendix VI.

we based them upon a moral comment which was both ungenerous and untrue. And when the Germans contend that this has placed us in a false position from the outset they are abundantly correct.'

This charge of 'hypocrisy' has often been made, though not usually with Mr. Nicolson's violence of language; and we must ask whether its harshness is justified either by the facts or by the terms of the Note itself.

The 'colonial guilt' charge was an exaggeration and, in our opinion, an unfortunate exaggeration, though of a kind not uncommon in the embittered circumstances of the time. It laid all the emphasis on the errors and scandals of Germany's early colonial period, when she was by no means the only offender; and it gave no credit for the conscientious effort which Germany had made, in the comparatively brief period after 1907, to set her house in order. To that extent we agree with Mr. Nicolson that it was ungenerous and untrue. If it was meant to convey that Germany, *as a nation*, alone of all first-class European powers, was unfit to be entrusted with the government of backward peoples, we do not think it sustainable either in 1919 or at the present time; though it must be added that, to many minds, what is true of the German nation as such is not necessarily true of the German nation under its present rulers and its present political doctrines. All this admitted, it is doubtful whether the indictment was a piece of deliberate hypocrisy rather than a belief sincerely held at the time, though

The Peace Settlement and the Mandates System 45

biased, as was not unnatural in the circumstances, by an inclination to dwell more on Germany's failures than successes in the colonial sphere. It is always easy to be self-righteous about the self-righteousness of twenty years ago. Nevertheless, we do not feel that the 'guilt' charge is one which should be maintained to-day, nor do we think any colonial Power so blameless, at all periods of its history, that it can level unqualified reproaches at others without danger of recrimination.

As for the rest of the Note, it is to be observed that the Allies very frankly state their intention 'to safeguard their own security and the peace of the world against a military imperialism', and assert that the economic importance of her colonies to Germany is largely fictitious. Far from being 'hypocritical', these arguments, in our opinion, were valid in 1919, and, as we show elsewhere, are equally valid to-day.

Much has been made of the 'hypocritical' inconsistency between the secret treaties concerning the colonies (see *ante*, pp. 21–2) and the principles of the Fourteen Points. There certainly was an inconsistency, but it cannot be regarded as Machiavellian, since all the secret treaties were made before the Fourteen Points were formulated or even contemplated. The treaties were of a kind common enough between allies in all wars; we may consider them as belonging to an evil military tradition, but such was the tradition upon which the War was fought, and the treaties are not rendered 'hypocritical' because President Wilson afterwards attempted to found a different tradition.

There is more ground for alleging casuistry in the subsequent process of fitting the existing bargains into the framework of Mr. Wilson's idealistic generalities; yet, as we have seen, Mr. Wilson himself became convinced that it was unwise and impracticable to hand back the newly conquered territories to Germany, and was satisfied that the compromise of Mandates sufficiently fulfilled the spirit of his Point 5.

Finally, is it true to say that the Allies were guilty of hypocrisy because they did not 'frankly annex these territories by right of conquest'? Without wishing to attribute to belligerents higher motives than they usually possess, we question whether pure materialism would have represented the true attitude of the victorious Powers any more accurately than pure altruism. In 1919 a great wave of hope succeeded a tempest of despair; there was widespread belief that war had succeeded in ending war, and that the new and inspiring conception of the League of Nations inaugurated a new world order, which would expel the old territorial greed, along with many other evils, from a chastened civilization. It would be, at best, a half-truth to say that the tutelary Powers accepted their Mandates in a cynical spirit, as veiled spoils. In twenty years the world has, unhappily, been forced to abandon many of its illusions, but it would be a mistake to attribute to 1919 the wearied cynicism of 1939. Apart from that, we do not think that the trusteeship which was the essence of the Mandate system was insincerely conceived or has been insincerely discharged.

III

ECONOMIC ARGUMENTS

I

THE demand for the return of Germany's colonies was not created by the National Socialist Party. From 1919 onwards various organizations, such as the German Colonial Society, which had 250 branches and 30,000 members by 1926, and the group in the Reichstag known as the Colonial Committee, worked to keep the issue still alive. On the whole, however, it was not a great popular movement: its chief adherents were men who had had experience in or knowledge of the colonies before the War, men like Dr. Seitz, former Governor of South West Africa, and Dr. Schnee, former Governor of German East Africa. The mass of the German people was too much concerned with the problems of unemployment and inflation to care very much about colonies.

The policy of the Nazi party has been to arouse the maximum of public interest in the colonial question. With all the resources of their propaganda technique the present German leaders have stimulated 'the spontaneous expression of the natural desire for the re-acquisition of colonies', and the demand for return has of late been given special prominence in the Nazi political programme. The Nazis have not always shown this enthusiasm for colonies. In *Mein Kampf* a number of passages can be found which point very much the other way. Thus in the 1930 edition Herr Hitler writes:

'It is not to colonial acquisition that we must look for a solution of this question (extension of Germany's "living-room") but exclusively to the acquisition of territory for settlement which will increase the area of the motherland.' (p. 741.)

'We finally part with the colonial and trade policy of the period before the War and pass over to the land policy of the future.' (p. 742.)

'Take every care that the strength of our people has its foundations not in colonies, but in the land of its home in Europe.' (p. 754.)[1]

There has been a division of opinion within the Nazi party itself, a section of which seems to have been opposed to colonial expansion. After 1934 this division became less and less important and by 1936 the colonial school, of whom General von Epp was one of the more prominent leaders, had established its supremacy. More and more frequent became the colonial references in important speeches, and Nazi penetration was actively pursued in South West Africa and more unobtrusively in Tanganyika.

Although no official demand has yet been made by the German Government for the return of colonies, we have by now become accustomed to a barrage of semi-official propaganda. What are the arguments with which the German spokesmen support their claims? For the sake of convenience we have followed the customary, but sometimes artificial, division of these

[1] Quoted with other passages in *Germany's Claim to Colonies*, p. 25.

arguments into political and economic: in this section only the economic arguments are considered. These are three in number. First, it is said that Germany lacks nearly all the principal raw materials and foodstuffs necessary to a highly industrial country, and that the return of her former colonies would ease her difficulties in this respect. Secondly, the possession of colonies would, according to the German view, provide her with additional markets for her products. Thirdly, it is argued, that with colonial territories at her disposal, Germany could free herself from the pressure of over-population. These are the three arguments which we now propose to consider.

II

The background to all Germany's demands is her peculiar economic system: only in this setting can their force be appreciated.[1] That system is dominated by two aims—the state's complete control of the whole economic life of the nation, and the attempt to achieve self-sufficiency. The extent to which the state has already taken economic control is amazing: foreign trade, wages, prices, production, labour-conditions, hours of work, organization of employers and employees, diversion of industry into new channels, the providing of capital—all are controlled in one way or another by the state. Only one gap remains to be filled before that control can be complete: Germany

[1] For a recent clear discussion of the system, see *The Round Table*, December 1938: 'The Economic Régime of the Third Reich.'

must import raw materials, which she lacks herself, and, since the Government cannot control world prices, here is a variable factor which the state cannot stabilize as it would wish. The struggle for self-sufficiency is thus an attempt to render Germany independent of those factors—such as the rise and fall of world prices—which are beyond her rulers' control, and to make her invulnerable against the threat of economic sanctions and blockade in time of war.

Could Germany obtain the raw materials she needs for her industries—particularly her armament industries—without having to buy them from foreign countries, the economic dictatorship of the Nazi Government would be complete. This explains the intensity of the Nazi drive for self-sufficiency. Other countries besides Germany lack supplies of the basic raw materials in their own territory, but only those countries in which the state aims at economic dictatorship feel the urgency which, on political no less than on economic grounds,[1] is apparent in the German Government's attitude to this question.

A brief examination of Tables I and II will show the truth of German complaints about the lack of raw materials in their own territories. Certain differences have been made since 1936 when Table I was compiled, by the annexation of Austria and Czechoslovakia, but the difference is not sufficient to

---

[1] For a full discussion of the whole raw materials situation, see *Raw Materials and Colonies* (R.I.I.A., 1936) and Alfred Plummer, *Raw Materials or War Materials?* (Gollancz, London, 1937).

Economic Arguments

change the general position. The Table shows that the resources of the British Empire as a whole, of the U.S.A., and the U.S.S.R. are all relatively complete, though there are gaps in each case—e.g. rubber, tin, and other metals in the U.S.A. and in the U.S.S.R. It is important to note that Great Britain, within her own territory, has only abundant supplies of coal: her deficiencies are met partly by the resources of the colonial empire, but much more by those of the Dominions and India. Of the other major powers France, within her own territory, has iron, potash, bauxite, and flax. Her colonial empire supplies certain needs, but she has insufficient coal, rubber, lead, and zinc, and no petroleum or cotton. Italy's position is very little improved by her colonial possessions: she has surplus supplies of silk, hemp, mercury, and sulphur, and sufficient lead, zinc, bauxite, and vegetable oils. Her lack of coal is being met to a certain extent by hydro-electric development. If Japan succeeds in maintaining control of North China her position will be materially improved by the mineral deposits there: as it is, she is better supplied than either Germany or Italy, although still inadequately. The three remaining countries, Belgium, Czechoslovakia,[1] and Poland, are all in much the same position as the 'dissatisfied Powers'. The Congo can supply Belgium only with copper, tin, and vegetable oils: otherwise Belgium can meet none of her requirements.

Germany can satisfy her own demands for coal and

[1] Written before the annexation of Czechoslovakia in March, 1939.

potash,[1] but whereas Great Britain's deficiencies are covered by the resources of the colonial empire and the Dominions, Germany has no overseas territories upon which to draw. She thus emerges as one of the most poorly supplied countries on the list; and this she regards as a startling position for one of the leading political and industrial powers in the world. Of the basic industrial raw materials—coal, iron, oil, cotton, and rubber—she possesses only the first. So far we must admit that Germany has some cause for dissatisfaction.

But it is a large step from admitting that Germany is poorly provided with raw materials to concluding that therefore her former colonies should be returned to her. Even on the facts so far adduced it is clear that Germany is by no means the only country with inadequate resources. Two countries alone can claim to be relatively self-sufficient—the U.S.A. and the U.S.S.R. To give the appearance of British self-sufficiency it is necessary, first, to assume that Great Britain can keep her sea routes open and, secondly, to include the self-governing Dominions and India, and their independence in economic matters is far more real than is sometimes realized. Great Britain is far more completely dependent upon imports of food from foreign countries than any other European nation. 9,341,797 tons of wheat, barley, and maize were imported in

[1] The annexation of Austria and Czechoslovakia has added to Germany's coal-resources and met her needs for magnesite, graphite, and antimony. It also reduces her deficiencies of iron, timber, and mercury.

1937: 35 per cent. of the wheat, 76 per cent. of the barley, 90 per cent. of the maize came from countries outside the British Empire and the Dominions. The problem of raw materials is not a German problem alone: it is an international problem, touching many countries in varying degrees. We hear most of German and Italian grievances, but it is well to remember that Belgium and Poland, to take only two instances, also have their difficulties.

Nor does it necessarily follow that the possession of colonies would solve the problem. In Table III the proportions of colonial productions of raw materials are shown.[1] Examination of this Table shows that the importance of the colonies as producers of raw materials is far less than might be expected. Rubber, it is true, is virtually a colonial monopoly; vegetable oils, tin, graphite, and phosphates, and foodstuffs like cocoa, tea, cane sugar, bananas, and vegetable fats, come largely from colonial territories, but otherwise they are relatively unimportant. The most important producers of the principal industrial raw materials are independent states. Thus the proportions of iron, lead, and coal produced in the colonies are too small to figure on the list: their exports of petroleum, zinc, mercury, silk, cotton, wool, and flax are little larger,

[1] The figures given in all these Tables are only approximate. It is practically impossible for Tables on so large a scale to present absolutely correct figures, a difficulty freely recognized in other similar publications. The figures are, however, all obtained from official sources, and the necessary qualifications as to dates, &c., stated: within a reasonable margin of error the figures are correct and show the broad outlines of the situation.

and only small quantities of the staple foodstuffs of western Europe—wheat, barley, dairy products, and meat—come from the colonies.

Among the different colonial areas two colonies are outstanding for their production of raw materials—Malaya and Netherlands India. Germany's former territories are, without exception, insignificant; their exports are analysed in Appendix III and it may be of interest to add that only 1 per cent. of Germany's vital imports of raw materials and 1 per cent. of her vital imports of foodstuffs in 1912 came from her colonies. Figures given in *The Colonial Problem* (pp. 291–2) show that France alone of the great colonial powers is dependent to any marked extent upon imports from her colonies: in 1935 10 per cent. of her imported raw materials and 65·5 per cent. of her imported foodstuffs came from her colonial possessions, although the latter figure is deceptive, because France, herself an agricultural country, produces a larger proportion of her own food than most countries. A similar analysis of figures shows for the United Kingdom 7·9 per cent. of food and tobacco, and 11·1 per cent. of raw materials imported from the colonies (excluding the Dominions) in 1935; and for Belgium in 1933 1·4 per cent. of foodstuffs, 3·7 per cent. of raw materials.[1]

It is difficult to avoid the conclusion that the importance of colonies as producers of raw materials and foodstuffs has been exaggerated. They produce a

[1] See Table IV for later figures, not distinguishing between raw materials and foodstuffs.

Economic Arguments

striking variety of different foodstuffs and raw materials, but for the most part in small quantities. Both England and France supplement their resources of raw materials by imports from the colonies, but in neither case do those imports represent much more than one-tenth of their total imports. If this is true of colonial possessions in general, it is very much more true of the ex-German colonies.[1] Figures show that if the total production of the former German colonies were diverted to Germany it would supply all Germany's requirements of sisal, three-quarters of its phosphates, one-third of its cocoa, one-fifth of its tropical woods, and a quantity of gold and diamonds, together with smaller proportions of certain other products, such as vanadium from South West Africa. Altogether, this is not a very comprehensive list. It is certainly true, as the Germans urge, that present production does not necessarily indicate potential production: in very few African countries has there been any thorough geological surveying. This point must not be overlooked: on the other hand, it can easily be exaggerated. Exploiting new resources, even where they exist, is a slow process; it means big initial outlay of capital without much immediate return and, unless carefully safeguarded, it may mean disaster for the native population. Granted that potentialities are far greater than actual production it is still practically impossible that her former colonies should ever supply the greater part of Germany's raw material needs.

[1] See Appendix III.

The promised land may flow with milk and honey: for the more material needs, however, of a nation which prefers guns to butter its resources are singularly disappointing.

In any case, is it true that territorial control is necessary for access to raw materials? In 1935 Germany took a relatively large proportion of her former colonies' exports, despite the fact that they were no longer under her political control: 81 per cent. of the exports from the British Cameroons, 19 per cent. from French Togo, 13 per cent. from South West Africa, 14 per cent. from Nigeria, and 8 per cent. from Tanganyika.[1] Because in Germany all economic life is directed and dominated by the state, it does not necessarily follow that this is so in other countries. In the colonies it is true to say that, with certain exceptions, their exports can be bought by any nation; thus Malaya finds her chief customer in the U.S.A.; in 1934 only 18·9 per cent. of her exports went to the United Kingdom, and some of these were re-exported.[2] The same situation exists in Netherlands India, the other great colonial producer besides Malaya. Since the War the raw materials market has been affected by a glut of over-production rather than by any scarcity: since 1929, owing to the drop in prices, any purchaser is welcomed, without discrimination. Sir Samuel Hoare, speaking at Geneva, in 1935 remarked: 'My impression is that there is no question in present circumstances of any colony withholding its raw

[1] *The Colonial Problem*, p. 293. [2] Ibid., p. 317.

Economic Arguments

materials from any purchaser. On the contrary, the trouble is that they cannot be sold at remunerative prices.' If this is true of the colonies, it is even more true of those independent states which, as we have seen, are the most important producers of raw materials. Mr. Plummer summed up the situation justly when he wrote:[1]

'Apart from import duties, quotas, and other restrictions imposed by their own governments, the German, Italian, and Japanese manufacturers of cotton and woollen fabrics are as free to buy American, Egyptian, and Indian raw cotton, Australian, New Zealand, Indian, or American wool at prevailing world prices as the textile manufacturers of Lancashire, Yorkshire, or Northern France. The same is true of almost every other branch of industry. The necessity to import basic raw materials from foreign countries is not a new economic phenomenon, nor need it be a hindrance to successful industrial development in the importing country. The past prosperity of the British cotton manufacturers was not frustrated by the fact that the raw cotton had to be bought from foreigners, nor was the British steel industry ruined when it became necessary to import iron ore from Sweden or Spain.'

If this were not true in general, it would be impossible to explain how such a country as Belgium, for instance, without adequate resources in her own territory, continues to supply her industries, and to hold an important place among the industrial powers of the world. Are there, then, any particular reasons

[1] Op. cit., p. 18.

why Germany should not enjoy equal access to raw materials with other countries? Such obstacles, if they exist, might be of two kinds: direct, in the shape of definite restriction or discrimination; or indirect, caused by difficulty of payment, and in particular by the lack of foreign exchange. We propose to consider the direct obstacles first and to divide these into three sections.

A. *Discriminatory Export Duties.* In certain countries, particularly those which are under-developed, and where there are few sources of taxation, export duties are imposed to yield revenue. Their proportions are, however, moderate, and since the authorities are in such cases naturally inclined to increase rather than to restrict trade, they can be left out of our reckoning. The only two serious cases of genuine discrimination appear in the French and Portuguese colonies: Lisbon has owed its prosperity largely to its position as the principal entrepôt for export for the Portuguese colonies and the French have encouraged colonial export to France by preferential export duties, recently increased by a system of bounties (*primes de compensation*) which protect the colonial producer against any sharp fall in the world market.

Neither the French nor the Portuguese, however, possess in their colonies anything like a monopoly of any raw material, and in the other colonial empires—the Dutch, the Japanese, the Belgian, and the American outlying territories (except the Virgin Islands)—such duties are rarely, if ever, imposed.

Economic Arguments

In the British colonial empire only three instances are found: tin from the Straits Settlement or Nigeria is subject to a prohibitive duty unless it is to be smelted in British territory, and from 1919 to 1922 palm-kernels exported from British West Africa were charged a heavy discriminatory duty, now abandoned.

The exports of Spanish Guinea, Italian Libya, and Somaliland are too insignificant to make their heavy duties at all important; but a word may be said about the mandated ex-German colonies. In A and B Mandates equality of access is secured by the mandates' constitutions, and is enjoyed by any country which cares to buy there: Germany is, in fact, a considerable purchaser from her former colonies. In C Mandates this equality is not guaranteed: other countries besides the mandatories do buy from them, but not to any considerable extent. Again, their exports are too small to make this of much importance. The only conspicuous case of monopoly is Nauru with its phosphates, and even there small exports are made to Japan and Finland.[1]

B. *Restriction on Investment.* Freedom of access, as the R.I.I.A. report on *Raw Materials and Colonies* points out, implies the right to exploit as well as to purchase colonial raw materials on equal terms. Practice again varies from empire to empire. On the one side are the Dutch and British colonies where there are few restrictions on foreign investments. Only in the case of petroleum in British colonies and mining in Dutch is

[1] See figures for mandated territories in Appendix III.

there discrimination. In British Malaya rubber is cultivated by companies known to be under Japanese, American, Belgian, French, Danish, and Italian control. American capital is invested in companies producing manganese in the Gold Coast, petroleum in Trinidad, and bauxite in British Guiana. In Netherlands India, of the capital invested in rubber 56 per cent. is foreign, in tea 30 per cent., in palm-oil 46 per cent.[1] To a certain extent capital will inevitably follow the flag and investors in countries which own colonies will naturally enjoy opportunities—and guarantees—which those in other countries cannot share. But there is at least no deliberate exclusion.

On the other hand, in the Japanese and French colonial empires foreign capital is not welcomed and, despite treaty provisions, the Belgian Congo is largely run by Belgian companies. Here a definite policy is followed of reserving opportunities for investment to nationals of the metropolitan state. In the C Mandates a similar policy is pursued, Nauru again being a striking example.

It does not necessarily follow that such restriction on investments means restriction on access to raw materials. It is possible to conceive of a company, financed by Dutch or Belgian capital, and exploiting the resources of Dutch or Belgian territory, yet willing, even eager, to sell to other countries. Whether, in fact, the companies which control the production of

[1] Figures taken from R.I.I.A. report, *Raw Materials and Colonies*, pp. 47–8.

Economic Arguments

raw materials do pursue monopolistic trade policies is a question which must be answered in Section C.

C. *International Restriction Schemes.* Although supplies of a certain raw material may lie within the territory of a state, it does not by any means follow that that state controls their exploitation. In most cases the companies concerned are privately, not publicly, owned and are financed by private capital. We must again insist that the position of the state in German economic life is exceptional; the stock reproach in most countries is that private capital controls the state, not vice versa. This being so, we may expect to find the producers of any one raw material grouped together in some international cartel and practising restriction of production irrespective of the national interests or the national policy of any state. It is probably in this way that the greatest obstacles to free access to raw materials are created.[1]

Mr. Plummer has made a thorough survey of international restriction schemes in his book, *Raw Materials or War Materials?* (Gollancz, London, 1937). We do not propose to overburden the argument with statis-

---

[1] In Sections A and B we confined our review to the colonies. Naturally, when raw materials are found within the territory of a sovereign state, it will have the first call upon its own supplies, and exploitation will be principally undertaken by home companies. But in the case of international restriction schemes, this distinction between independent states and colonies no longer applies. The principal supplies of raw materials are found in independent states and producers in independent states are involved as much as, if not considerably more than, colonial producers in these international cartels.

tical material, but simply to draw certain conclusions, referring the reader to Mr. Plummer's book and to Appendix IV of *Raw Materials and Colonies* for a fuller presentation of the figures.

During the last few years, since the depression of the early thirties, international cartels have been attempted, or are still in existence, dealing with the production of the following raw materials:

Wheat, sugar;

Tin, zinc, lead, bauxite;

Mercury, sulphur, potash, nitrates (and manufactured nitrogen), petroleum, rubber.

The great expansion in production after the War, combined with the fall of prices and the contraction of demand during the world depression, created a situation in which control of some sort became an imperative necessity. The schemes which were devised aimed only at securing a reasonable price for the producer without treating the consumer unfairly, and in the majority of cases a just and moderate policy has been adhered to.

In only two important cases did Mr. Plummer find that prices had been raised to a level at which the producer reaped monopolistic profit: these were the copper cartel, which lasted from 1926 until 1932, when it collapsed; and the organization which curtails the production of tin ore. These attempts to limit production are always precarious, partly because of the difficulty of making the scheme universal and enforcing the restrictions, partly because such schemes are always an incentive to develop new sources of production (e.g. the effect of the 1926–32 copper cartel upon the exploitation of Rhodesian copper deposits). The high prices and scarcity of petrol, wheat, and sugar in Germany and Italy, it may be of interest to add, are due far more to government attempts to achieve self-sufficiency than to any international control schemes. Thus the price of wheat in Italy was 110 lire per quarter in 1932, when imported wheat without the duty would have cost 49 lire,[1] and in Berlin (June 1931) wheat was 7s. 3d. per bushel at a time when its price in the open market was 3s. 2½d.[2] In Italy, again, a tax of 2s. per gallon on imported petrol was paid by Italian consumers to protect, in the interests of self-sufficiency, a home petrol industry capable in the peak year of 1933 of supplying 2 per cent. of Italy's petrol consumption. Similar measures for the protection of the home sugar-beet industry have been instituted in Germany.

So far as direct restrictions are concerned, the conclusion would appear to be that these do not constitute serious obstacles in the way of Germany's access to raw materials. Restrictions, we have seen, do exist, but their effect is principally one of irritation, and their extent can easily be exaggerated. That France and Portugal discriminate, in their colonies, in favour of exports to the mother country appears a less sinister

[1] R.I.I.A. *Report on Economic and Financial Position of Italy*, p. 34, quoted in Plummer.
[2] *Economic Journal*, Dec. 1931: quoted in Plummer, op. cit.

fact when one adds that, after all, neither the French nor the Portuguese colonies enjoy a monopoly in the production of any raw material. Similarly when one is tempted to expatiate on the iniquities of international restriction schemes, it is well to remember that the producers have often a strong case to put in their own defence and that Great Britain or France suffers as much as Germany from monopolistic prices. Certainly, there is nothing like discrimination against Germany alone in this matter.

Before summing up the arguments about raw materials, we have still to consider the German argument that Germany is at a particular disadvantage owing to difficulties of payment caused by the lack of foreign exchange. This is, in many ways, the strongest part of the German case on economic grounds; as such it deserves careful consideration. The argument runs thus: Germany is a poor country, with slender stocks of foreign exchange and gold. Between May 1931 and September 1938 the Reichbank's reserves in gold and foreign exchange fell from 2,576 to 76 million marks. Germany is unable to replace this loss of income from foreign investments or by foreign loans, which it is difficult for the Nazi Government to raise; she can only acquire foreign currency with which to pay for raw material imports by trade;[1] but trade is impeded by mounting tariff barriers all over the world. The

[1] By Articles 120–5 and 257–60 of the Treaty of Versailles Germany lost her investments in the mandated territories. According to Dr. Townsend 505 million marks German and 88 million marks foreign capital were invested in the German colonies.

Economic Arguments

only way out of an impossible position, according to Dr. Schacht, is for Germany to possess within her own monetary system colonial territories from which she can draw raw materials, paying for them in her own currency, and without recourse to her already depleted stock of foreign exchange.

Undoubtedly there is force in Dr. Schacht's argument, but it tends to over-simplify a complicated situation. It is certainly not fair to lay the whole blame for the present depression in international trade upon countries like Germany and Italy, which have pursued the mirage of self-sufficiency. As the R.I.I.A. report on *Raw Materials and Colonies* pointed out:

'The American tariff and the French quotas have had far more disastrous international effects than the barriers erected in reply by Germany and Italy: the fact that these two creditor countries have now accumulated two-thirds of the world's gold reserves is a sure sign that they have not been balancing their international payments and receipts.'[1]

On the other hand German policy has not made matters any easier. In an attempt to maintain an artificially high level for the national currency she has erected elaborate exchange barriers which prevent the mark from finding its natural level, and thus handicap the export industries by keeping their prices artificially high in terms of foreign currencies and making all trade with Germany an immensely com-

[1] Op. cit., p. 35.

plicated procedure. Again, the German subordination of economic to military interests produces further needless difficulties. This subordination appears, first in the ruthless drive for self-sufficiency, and secondly in the re-armament programme; the exceptional demand of the armament industries for raw materials has aggravated the exchange shortage, greatly reduced the import of foodstuffs, and limited the productive capacity of the export industries.

Nor does it follow that the best way of solving Germany's difficulties is the return of her former colonies. Certainly for such raw materials as she drew from them Germany would be able to pay in her own currency, but, as we have seen, it would be virtually impossible for Germany ever to satisfy her raw material demands, or even any large part of them, from those territories. The real problem is not a colonial one, and is not to be solved by the transfer of colonial possessions. It is essentially an international problem —how to remove the present crippling restrictions from world trade—and it can only be solved by international action. Against such action the German Government seems resolutely to have set its face: the return of her colonies, it is frankly admitted, would be the prelude not to a move for freer trade, but to an intensification of the tariff system. Germany can, therefore, scarcely complain if the other Powers are slow to help her when by doing so they will only increase their own difficulties.

At the risk of repetition it may be worth while to

Economic Arguments

summarize the conclusions to which we came after an examination of these arguments. It is true that Germany was very poorly supplied with raw materials in her own territory; but we found that few, if any, states could claim to be self-sufficient in this respect. The importance of the colonies as producers of raw materials appears to have been exaggerated; the transfer of colonial territories could not solve the problem of supply because the most important producers of raw materials are independent states. Distasteful though it may be to her rulers, Germany will have to rely for her stocks of the principal raw materials, like practically all the other states, upon foreign trade. Accepting this situation we then asked whether there were any particular obstacles which prevented Germany having access to raw-material markets by the normal process of trade. We found that such restrictions as did exist were not of great importance, and that there was no peculiar discrimination against Germany. As for German exchange difficulties, we saw little reason to believe that the return of her former colonies and the creation of a 'mark-area' there would provide a remedy, which must be sought in the liberation of international trade from its present crippling restrictions (for which Germany is not responsible) and in the adoption of a more liberal economic policy in Germany. The production of raw materials in her former colonies is far too small to make their return appear as anything like a solution to Germany's raw-materials problem.

Economic Arguments

The division between economic and political arguments, though convenient, is at times artificial; and this examination of the economic side of the raw-materials problem would be incomplete without mentioning two of the political issues directly involved. In the first place, it is easy to forget that the exploitation of the colonies is not only an economic but also a human question. Those who are certain to be most deeply affected by any transfer of colonial territories to meet Germany's economic difficulties are the native peoples. It is clear from the statement of the German leaders that, should their ex-colonies be returned to them, they contemplate a swift and immediate development of their material resources. It cannot be too strongly insisted upon that such a policy could be pursued only at the risk of disaster to the native population. The land to be exploited, the labour for its development would have to be provided by the natives: their interests, like the interests of the German working-class, would necessarily be sacrificed to the paramount claims of the state to the end that production might be increased. The German working-class may—or may not—think the game is worth the candle; there is no reason why the African should. Certainly, the British have not a blameless record in this respect, but they are beginning to learn from their mistakes, they are not driven by the same necessity as the Nazis, and in the mandated ex-German colonies, at any rate, they are restrained by their obligations to the League, obligations which it is sheer delusion to imagine the present German Government would accept. Before one decides that return of her colonies is the only way to meet Germany's economic difficulties it is well to remember that other interests besides those of the Great Powers are involved in the deal.[1]

Secondly, any discussion of raw materials and the difficulties of certain states in obtaining them becomes unreal, unless one recognizes that over the whole debate there lies the shadow of war. Germany does not possess within her own territory adequate resources for a war of any duration, and it has been frequently suggested that it is for this reason that Germany desires sources of raw materials under her own political control and finds the alternative of freer international trade and an extension of the 'Open Door' an unsatisfactory remedy.[2]

One can well understand the German fear of econo-

[1] For the extraordinary complexity of the problems of colonial, especially African development, the reader is referred to *The Colonial Problem*, pp. 109–275; Woolf, *Empire and Commerce in Africa*; Olivier, *White Capital and Coloured Labour*; I. C. Greaves, *Modern Production among Backward Peoples*; and the writings of Mr. Leonard Barnes.

[2] Herr Hitler in his speech to the Reichstag of 20 February 1938 said: 'I should like to turn here against the hope that such claims (i.e. for colonies) can be averted by granting credits. We do not want credits, but a foundation to live which will enable us to secure national existence by our own industriousness. Above all, we do not wish for naïve assurances that we shall be permitted to buy what we need. We reject such statements once and for all; they are regarded in our country as nothing but sheer mockery. There exists no recipe in world economics which can offer a full substitute for the possibility of an intensive economic system within a territory having the same currency.'

mic sanctions and blockade. But in the present unstable international situation, when, after the experience of September 1938, we know that war, however bloody, futile, and horrible it may appear to the majority of people, is no longer unthinkable, we are forced to ask: Is it wise to throw away one of our greatest advantages, to give a possible antagonist easier access to the supplies of raw materials with which he may build armaments to defeat us? We feel no pleasure in asking such a question, but we realize that it is not to be ignored in considering the German arguments. None of us feel much satisfaction with the post-War policy of France and Great Britain towards Germany, which has substantially contributed to the present situation: there is truth in the German argument that if Great Britain and France dislike the present policy of the Reich, they have done little in the past to make alternative policies practicable. But there comes a time when questions of blame and recrimination must take second place to the question of survival. The attitude of the German Government affords no comfort or security. Herr Hitler appears to have little use for a policy of conciliation and co-operation, except on his own terms. He may frighten the other Powers into making concessions which will ease Germany's economic straits: he can scarcely expect that they will of their own accord strengthen the German economic position when by so doing they only weaken their own chances in another war. Herr Hitler possesses to-day greater power to free the world

Economic Arguments

from the terrible threat of war than any other man: if he will make use of that opportunity the solution of Germany's economic problems will not be unobtainable. Until then it is as reasonable for the Powers to refuse the German demands, in fear of another war, as it is for the German Government, also in fear of war, to make them.

III

The second German argument for the return of her colonies on economic grounds is the benefit she would derive from having a secure market for her export industries in her overseas possessions. It is as well to clear away a possible misunderstanding at the outset: increased trade with her own colonies would not give Germany a greater supply of foreign exchange, because, *ipso facto*, her colonial subjects would pay for their purchases in German marks. But if Germany had political control of her former colonies, their foreign trade would be controlled by Germany and consequently her stocks of foreign currency would be increased. There would be an increase in the total amount of German trade with foreign countries. The increase, however, would be small and such economic relief as it brought would be temporary.

Most people are surprised to learn that colonial trade accounts only for about 11 per cent. of the total trade of the world; as in the production of raw materials, so in international trade the independent states[1]

[1] Including the Dominions and India as independent states, not as part of the colonial empire, because they are self-governing.

are much more important than the colonial areas. Table IV shows the importance of their own colonial trade for each of the great colonial Powers: it figures most prominently in the trade of France and Japan, though the addition of the Dominions' Trade makes clear the importance of the imperial connexion to Great Britain. The extremely small figure for the German empire in 1913 does not perhaps do full justice to their case. As Dr. Schacht pointed out in *Foreign Affairs* (January 1937), the difference between pre-War and post-War is all-important. Before the War there was free trade over a far wider area than there is to-day. With the rapid development of tariff systems since the War the area of free trade has shrunk to very small dimensions and in relation to this the possession of secure, closed colonial markets has become of greater significance and value.

Leaving aside the question of tariff barriers in the great independent states such as the U.S.A. and France, it is worth while to consider how far the foreign exporter is being excluded from the colonial market in favour of the producer in the metropolitan country. *The Colonial Problem* (pp. 298–306) contains an analysis of the present tariff policies of the great colonial powers. In practically every case the justice of the complaint that the foreign exporter is being excluded appears to be unquestionable. For the British Empire the Import Duties Act, 1932, and the Ottawa Agreements of 1932 meant a definite break with the traditional policy of free trade and the estab-

Economic Arguments

lishment of a system of imperial preference,[1] covering the whole of the British Empire. In France, the policy of protection is of older standing and the Law of 13 April 1928 was only one in a long series of protective measures. By this enactment the colonies (except those in North Africa) are divided into two groups: first, the 'assimilated' colonies[2] in which the customs tariffs of France herself are applicable, and second, the other colonies, in which local tariffs are fixed by decrees adopted on the advice of the Minister for the Colonies and preference is given to French products. In Morocco France is obliged to maintain the 'Open Door' by the Algeciras Act, but Algiers has a complete, and Tunis practically a complete, customs union with the mother-country. Portugal, Italy, and Spain (except Spanish Morocco) all impose preferential tariffs in their colonies: Korea and Formosa are assimilated to the Japanese tariff system and the outlying territories of the U.S.A. to the American. Even the Dutch, long famous for their liberal trade policy, have been forced by the flow of Japanese imports into the East Indies to introduce quotas by the Crisis Import Ordinance of 1933, and Belgium, though precluded by international treaty obligations from erecting tariff barriers in the Congo or Ruanda-Urundi, in fact plays a predominant part in the trade of both territories.

[1] For examples of imperial preference tariffs in the British Empire, cf. *The Colonial Problem*, Appendix XI.
[2] Indo-China, Madagascar, West Indies, Réunion.

The result of all these restrictions can be seen in Table V which shows the amount of the colonies' trade with their metropolitan countries. These restrictions and preferences were not designed to discriminate against Germany in particular—Japan is more usually regarded as the sinister intruder by the colonial Powers—but in practice this does mean a reduction of the area of free trade for all countries without colonies. There are, of course, other factors besides tariff and quota schemes making for the predominance of the metropolitan countries in colonial trade—use of the same language and the same currency; established business connexions; the tendency for public contracts to be given to the mother-country;[1] the advantage of dealing through the great entrepôt towns of the mother-country—London and Liverpool in Great Britain, Rotterdam and Amsterdam in the Netherlands. Altogether, one may conclude that the complaint of exclusion from colonial trade is well founded.

Germany—and, we may add, the other non-colonial Powers—are naturally anxious about the future of their overseas markets, especially as the tendency towards protection appears to be increasing rather than slackening. We sympathize with that anxiety, but a colonial solution of the difficulties is barely practicable. The general economic situation

---

[1] In the British Colonial Development Act, 1929, it was provided that, as far as possible, the proceeds of colonial loans should be spent on empire products.

Economic Arguments 75

would not be improved, if—as seems probable—the return of her former colonies to Germany meant the conversion of an area of partial exclusion into an area of total monopoly. Nor would return do much to ease Germany's own economic difficulties. True, if Malaya and the Netherlands India, the two most profitable and best supplied colonial territories, were handed over to Germany, those difficulties would be materially reduced. That hypothesis is, of course, unthinkable. But the Germans and many of their sympathizers, when they speak of a colonial solution for their economic problems, seem habitually to think in terms of the wealth and resources of the British and Dutch colonial empires. A colonial solution in those terms is frankly impracticable: the only one which can possibly be considered is the return of the former German colonies, and these, despite Nazi optimism, are far from being another Malaya or Sumatra.

One has only to examine the present trade returns for the mandated territories to see that they offer a relatively negligible market for German exports. Moreover, whatever may be the situation in the rest of the British colonial empire, it is worth emphasizing that imperial preference schemes do not relate to A and B Mandates, where the open door is and must be maintained. This means that even at the moment Germany is in no way excluded from the markets of Tanganyika, the Cameroons, Togoland, and Ruanda-Urundi, though political control would naturally bring an increased share of trade.[1] We find, in short, the same situation as in the matter of raw materials. That Germany has genuine economic difficulties and just grievances is undeniable. Yet the solution appears to be, not the return of her former colonies, which are, comparatively speaking, economically negligible, but a return to freer international trade and especially the re-establishment of the 'Open Door' in the colonial areas. The return of her former colonies to Germany and the re-establishment of a German preferential tariff system in the colonies would be a step, not towards, but farther away from the solution of the world's economic difficulties.

We must beware, however, of hypocrisy. It is perfectly true that no nation, certainly not Germany, can be self-sufficient, either with or without colonies; that it is undesirable, from the point of view of every nation, that the world economy should be divided into closed compartments and restricted regional areas of trade; and that to restore to Germany her former colonies is to some extent to admit and to condone the trend towards restrictive colonial and world trade policies. But it is not for the British Government to use such arguments against return, unless it is prepared to accept their implication and to work hard for the removal of international restrictions to trade. If we have to assume that there may be a possible permanence and even an increasing development in tariff,

[1] See Appendix III for the value of German trade at the present time with her former colonies.

Economic Arguments

quota, and imperial preference systems, then it is plain hypocrisy for us to make the most of our colonial empire, but to refuse to hand back the German colonies on economic grounds. There may be the most cogent reasons for refusing to return them, but in such circumstances there would no longer be much validity in our economic arguments.

Note to Section III

Although it may seem a little irrelevant in a chapter on economic argument, it is noteworthy that there is sometimes a serious conflict between schemes of imperial preference and the idea of colonial trusteeship. We shall see that among the political arguments against return of the colonies, one of the most important is the claim that we are responsible for the welfare of the native peoples under our care and that we cannot betray their trust in us. The adverse effects of certain schemes of imperial preference upon native peoples is discussed in *The Colonial Problem* (pp. 311–13). In many cases they mean that the native has to pay more dearly for products which he needs, in others, that he simply cannot afford to pay the price and has to go without supplies altogether. An example of this is quoted in *The Round Table* (1934) from the Nairobi Correspondent of *The Times*. In East Africa the imposition of heavy duties makes it impossible for the native to buy the cheap Japanese rubber shoes. He cannot afford to pay the higher price for British products and must therefore go without: yet the medical authorities admit that the use of such cheap rubber shoes has done more to prevent hook-worm disease than all the efforts of their department. As a consequence, the standard of living declines and the burden of promoting intra-imperial trade falls heavily upon the colonial population.

Similarly the native producer may find that while he has lost his place in the world market owing to imperial preference and discriminating export duties, his products are unwelcome in the mother-country when they compete with home production. An instance of this is the cultivation of the vine and of wheat in French North Africa: in both cases the French Government has been forced to limit imports into France in the interests of French producers and, as a result, 'the native, bewildered at having first been encouraged to get the most out of his land, and then discouraged by a refusal to receive his crop, is at once discontented and reduced to poverty'.[1]

The tendency in intra-imperial trade schemes is to sacrifice the colonies to the interests of the metropolitan power. Thus colonial producers may be forced to adopt, against their wishes, an economy which is complementary to that of the mother-country, and in this way the advance to economic and political independence, which is the avowed aim of most powers holding their empires 'in trust', is retarded. Such considerations do not apply to A and B Mandates (though possibly to C Mandates), but they show that at times the doctrine of trusteeship wears a little thin, and thus they are relevant to the main discussion.

IV

The last of the main economic arguments with which Germany supports her claim for the return of her colonies is her need of an outlet for her surplus

[1] Speech by M. Rollin at the Conférence de la France Métropolitaine et d'Outremer, quoted in *The Colonial Problem*, pp. 311–12.

Economic Arguments

population, a need which the possession of her former colonies would, on the German view, adequately meet. This concept of a surplus population is elusive, and, as Sir Norman Angell has pointed out, is relative to the degree of industrialization which a country has obtained. Up to 1885 the Germans emigrated in large numbers, being second only to the British in the rate at which they left Europe. From then onwards, under the influence of direct government action, the number of emigrants steadily declined, and although the population of the Reich continued to increase, that increase was absorbed by the home country through greater industrialization. The result was that the German colonial empire was only very thinly settled with Europeans in 1914, there being in all only about 20,000 whites scattered through the different territories, the majority of them (11,000) in South West Africa.[1] The Germans, however, argue that to-day, since industrialization has proceeded almost to the maximum, the colonies would be looked at in a very different light and would be much more seriously developed. Hitherto, the U.S.A. has absorbed a large population of German emigrants (in 1930 there were 1,608,000 Germans among the foreign-born population of the U.S.A.): that flow is now checked by the strict American immigration laws and also by the unwillingness of the Nazi Government to let Germans escape from its close political

[1] For the distribution in the German colonial empire in 1914 see Appendix IV.

control. The general increase in such immigration restrictions since the War is a parallel to the erecting of tariff barriers in the sphere of trade, and has created considerable difficulties for many countries, e.g. Japan and Italy, besides Germany.

Many people tend to exaggerate the seriousness of Germany's population problem, not realizing that the problem is far greater in other countries, especially those of the Far East—India, China, and Japan. Even in Europe the density of population is higher in certain other countries than in Germany,[1] which appears to be faced with the general prospect of the countries of western Europe—a declining, or at best a stationary, birth-rate.

It is doubtful, moreover, whether a colonial solution of the problem is practicable to-day. A lucid summary of the position was given in *The Colonial Problem* (pp. 344–5) which we quote at length:

'Colonies do not offer any important remedy for population congestion in Europe, except perhaps in the Mediterranean countries of N. Africa. In the past European emigration on a large scale has been directed at non-colonial countries and above all to the Americas. The law of population-movement cannot be discussed here,[2] but it may be noted that the general trend of emigration is from regions with relatively low standards of living to those with higher standards. The primary object in emigration is individual betterment; disparity

[1] See figures in Table VI.
[2] A reference to Carr-Saunders, *World Population* (Oxford, 1936), is given.

Economic Arguments

in the standard of living, not disparity in population, is the driving force. Colonial areas were open to emigrants in the later years of the last century and up to the World War with practically no restrictions, but such emigrants as they attracted came mainly from the poorer countries, China, India, Arabia, and to some extent the Levant. They offered, and offer, no attraction to the European labourer or artisan, whose standard of living does not enable him to compete with the native. Emigration is directed to those countries where capital is increasing more rapidly than labour supply, as in North America in the heyday of development. A further condition is suitability of climate and social conditions, which tropical countries rarely offer to the European. In southern Africa and in Algeria before the War settlement was considerable, but, even in these otherwise suitable areas, the competition of a cheap local labour supply able to live on small wages has created the problem of the poor white. M. Armindo Monteiro, speaking at the opening session of the International Colonial Institute in 1933, drew a picture of the poverty and the "tragic situation which would be created by the transfer by a government of any considerable number of its citizens to colonial areas with the aim of solving the unemployment and poverty question at home. After the expenditure of fabulous sums they would merely have created a vast white proletariat in regions where it would be difficult to succour them". They would lack even the mutual support available in old settled countries.

'Consequently colonial opportunities, except for Eastern peoples, are of a limited character; they are for persons with directing ability and with capital, and they offer no large relief for congested populations.'

The truth of these statements is easily verifiable. Thus Great Britain, with all her great colonial possessions, has been unable to solve her unemployment problem by emigration. In the whole of tropical Africa, there are still only some 400,000 whites, even when a generous interpretation is given to that term: in the islands of Oceania (excluding Australia, New Zealand, and Hawaii) the white population is calculated at 113,000. The colonies are not empty areas; they contain vast native populations, frequently increasing; and the areas most suited to white settlement, especially in Africa, are already congested. Since, as we have already had occasion to remark, the former German colonies are not among the most favoured or the most attractive colonial territories, these general observations apply to them with considerable force. Appendix IV shows the present population of the mandated territories. In the second part of this book we shall examine the detailed possibilities of further settlement in each colony, but the general conclusion remains unshaken that settlement in her former colonies offers little prospect of relief to German social and economic problems, and that the German demand for return on these grounds is not strong enough to justify the transfer of the territories concerned.

V

Conclusion

We have not attempted to minimize the economic problems with which Germany is faced: they are real

Economic Arguments

and serious. But we do not feel that the return of her former colonies would substantially improve her position. A remedy must be sought elsewhere than in the colonial sphere—principally, we feel, in the direction of freer international trade, and closer international co-operation, as well as by a modification of Germany's present economic and political policies. For such changes in the international sphere the initiative cannot come from Germany alone, and we suggest that, if the governments of the other major Powers are impressed by the gravity of Germany's economic difficulties and feel an obligation to help, they should direct their efforts along this line of an international solution. Admittedly, if those colonies were returned, Germany would derive certain economic benefits from them, but those benefits are not sufficiently great to justify return upon economic grounds alone. These benefits would do little to solve the major German problems and, above all, they could be obtained only at a grave cost to the native population. We do not hesitate to say that, in our view, the economic arguments cannot be regarded as sufficient grounds for agreeing to return.

IV
POLITICAL ARGUMENTS
I

ALTHOUGH economic arguments are most frequently advanced in support of colonial claims, it is very doubtful whether these represent the real motives for colonial expansion. These are more likely to be sought with success in the political sphere. Fundamentally, the Germans look upon lack of colonies as a national grievance, a slur upon their national honour, a limitation of their claims to the prestige of a Great Power. Faced with shortages of food and raw materials, they find the economic arguments useful to allay discontent at home and divert its force to the creation of a sense of grievance against the Colonial Powers; but, although convenient, these arguments are not essential. Thus Dr. Nonnenbruch, Financial Editor of the *Völkischer Beobachter*, writes:

'The German standpoint—that her colonies have been taken by an act of force and therefore belong to her by right—is one of justice. As such it has little to do with economic considerations, even if, as is self-evident, we promise ourselves economic advantages from the possession of colonies. One thing is clear—the execution of the Four Year Plan will not be affected in any way by the colonial question, and, conversely, the colonial question is not affected by the execution of the Four Year Plan. That means . . . that the German right to colonies

Political Arguments

remains even if the problem of raw materials is solved for German industry.'[1]

We come now, therefore, to the most important, but also to the most difficult, part of the controversy; the most difficult, because on both sides we are faced with factors which are not susceptible of objective valuation, which cannot be assessed, like economic considerations, by a careful study of the facts. The position was lucidly put by the R.I.I.A. Report on *Germany's Claim to Colonies*:

'If considerations of prestige are the real driving force behind Germany's colonial campaign, then nothing less than the actual transfer of colonies—or possibly of Mandates—can be regarded by realists as likely to satisfy her; and among British people the idea of such a transfer immediately gives rise to ethical and emotional reactions. That is to say, it raises the question of justice and rouses the emotion of fear. What further complicates matters is the fact that neither the notion of justice nor the instinct of fear operates simply, either for or against the return of Germany's former colonies; both are double-edged. Justice for Germany is uppermost in some minds, justice for the natives under Great Britain's trusteeship in others. In the same way, fear of the strategic implications of colonial revision looms large for some people, while others are conscious of nothing so much as the danger of meeting Germany's claims with a blank *non possumus*' (pp. 51–2).

We are in no better position than other writers to give final answers to these questions; all that we can

---

[1] Quoted in *Germany's Claim to Colonies* (R.I.I.A., 1938), from the *Manchester Guardian* of 9 Dec. 1937.

do is to suggest what seem to us to be the important factors and to outline the considerations which determined our own answers to them. In editing the reports, we have found it convenient to split up the discussion into three sections, in each of which the focus of the arguments is different. The political aspect of the colonial problem is often discussed solely from an international point of view; but this, though highly important, is only one of several angles of approach. We have tried also to examine the situation from an imperial and from a colonial standpoint, to learn what would be the effects of transfer upon the British Empire as a whole and upon the territories themselves in such a readjustment. Especially, we wish to emphasize the importance of the colonial point of view. The words of the Introduction to *The Colonial Problem* are very pertinent:

> 'The controversy aroused by the international aspect of the colonial problem has thrown too great an emphasis upon purely territorial questions and has allowed the intricacy and diversity of the colonial problem as a whole and, especially, the relation between the governing and governed, to fall into the background. . . . The colonial problem cannot be reduced to some simplified conflict between the "haves" and "have nots", but is concerned with a process of dynamic development rather than with a static collection of territorial and economic facts' (p. 1).

Bearing this warning in mind, we propose to begin our examination of the political arguments from the colonial point of view.

II

If the German claims on the grounds of prestige and honour are to be satisfied by the transfer of colonial territories, it is obvious that the native population of those territories will be more deeply affected than any one else. We must attempt to get some clear idea of the precise effect upon them, and must ask whether the change will be to their advantage or disadvantage.

Naturally one first turns to the evidence available from the character of German rule up to 1914. At once, however, we are met with the bitter complaint that this evidence has rarely been stated with justice, that the facts have been twisted and presented in a 'garbled' version to serve as a justification for the action of the Allied Powers in 1919. The 'Colonial Guilt lie' was given its clearest expression in the Allied Note of 16 June 1919, the more important part of which has already been quoted in Chapter II[1]: in that Note the Allies refused to consider the return of her colonies to Germany on the grounds that she had been guilty of maladministration, with detrimental consequences to the interests of the natives. This accusation has had far-reaching effects: undoubtedly it has been widely believed in this country and bitterly resented in Germany. It is worth while, therefore, to consider briefly what justification there is for it, partly because this is one of the strongest of the German complaints, and partly because the attitude of the colonies towards return must be so strongly affected by its truth or falsehood.

[1] See also Appendix VI.

Political Arguments

Three distinct periods can be traced in the thirty years of Germany's colonial empire, each with different characteristics. The first lasted from 1884 to 1890, the second from 1890 to 1906, and the third from 1906 to 1914.[1]

(*a*) *1884–90*. It was very late in his career as Chancellor that Bismarck was converted to the doctrine of colonial expansion. Up to 1884 he believed that the European position of Germany, established by the two wars of 1866 and 1870–1 and the industrialization of the country, was too precarious to risk a diversion of her energies overseas. Bismarck habitually placed Germany's position in Europe before all other considerations, and, though in 1884 he extended the Government's protection to Nachtigal and Karl Peters in their advancement of German claims to territories in West and East Africa, he refused to allow the State to undertake direct responsibility for colonial administration. Dr. Townsend quotes[2] two statements by Bismarck on his policy:

'The German Empire cannot carry on a system like that of France. It cannot send out warships to conquer territories overseas, that is, it will not take the initiative: but it will protect the German merchant even in the land which he acquires. Germany will do what England has always done, establish Chartered Companies, so that the responsibility rests with them.

---

[1] For a brilliant and detailed examination of the German colonial empire, to which the Group owes a great deal, the reader is referred to *The Rise and Fall of the German Empire*, by Dr. M. E. Townsend (New York, 1930). [2] Op. cit., p. 119.

Political Arguments

'I would follow the example of England in granting to those merchants something like royal charters. I do not wish to found provinces, but to protect commercial establishments in their own development. We hope that the tree will flourish in proportion to the activity of the gardener, but, if it does not, the whole responsibility rests with him, and not with the Empire, which will lose nothing.'

From the German point of view Bismarck's creation of chartered companies was an ingenious device by which to promote national expansion. For the natives, however, the shifting of responsibility from the state to private companies, subject to no administrative control and interested only in making profits from their colonial adventures, was a disastrous policy. Every evil and abuse associated with the commercial exploitation of primitive peoples and lands was allowed to develop unchecked. The worst record is to be found in East Africa where the exploits of the adventurer Karl Peters caused a serious revolt in 1888 and forced the Imperial Government to intervene. Despite the fact that several of the companies enjoyed practically complete sovereign rights, they failed to achieve even the success of economic exploitation: in 1888 the South West Africa Co., in 1890 the East Africa Co., and in 1899 the New Guinea Co. all surrendered or lost their rights. Such a system, designed for the seventeenth century, failed to hold its own or to justify itself in the very different conditions of the nineteenth century. In every case the state had to assume the responsibility which it had attempted to avoid.

(b) *1890–1906*. The year 1890 saw the fall from power of the man who had dominated the German and the European scene for twenty years, Bismarck, and a consequent revolution in German foreign policy. Whereas Bismarck had always subordinated colonial policy to the exigencies of the European political system, Kaiser Wilhelm II pursued a grandiose and aggressive *Weltpolitik* for the naked and undisguised end of national prestige. The period is characterized by a series of crises in which Germany asserted her claims to a 'place in the Sun' in a blustering tone. The risks of this policy were lightly taken: Great Britain was flouted openly. In 1895–6 the Kaiser gave his open support to the Boers against England, finally sending the famous 'Kruger telegram', behind which lay his wish for active intervention—even, possibly, annexation. Thus, though the state had intervened to take over the colonies, it was a state which cared far more for prestige and military honour than for the responsibilities of colonial administration; it had no interest in the colonies themselves. Most of the colonial governors of this period were military men, unsympathetic, arrogant, and authoritarian: an elaborate bureaucratic system of control was set up, hopelessly inappropriate to a situation which required sympathy, insight, and adaptability in the administrators who had to deal with very primitive peoples. Above all, the economic development of the colonies was neglected and left in the hands of private capitalists who cared nothing for the welfare of the native peoples,

Political Arguments

were unrestrained by the Administration, and were content to exploit the territory with the minimum of responsibility. The result was a number of colonial scandals, which seriously discredited the service: Karl Peters in East Africa; Leist, governor of Kamerun; Wehlan, a judge in Kamerun; von Horn, governor of Togoland; von Puttkamer, governor of Kamerun; General Trotha, who suppressed the Herero rebellion in South West Africa—all men of a harsh and insensitive type, and all, except Trotha, convicted and dismissed for cruelty and maladministration.

(c) *1906–14*. The year 1906 was a turning-point in the history of the German colonial empire. While the imperialist and military clique in power was discredited by the colonial scandals, German public opinion was relentless in its criticism of the Government's colonial policy. The Socialists had always looked upon colonial expansion with dislike, as being another manifestation of the evils of capitalism: they were now joined in the Reichstag by the parties of the Centre and the *Freisinnige*—altogether a formidable opposition. From about 1904 onwards a fierce parliamentary campaign was waged on the colonial issue. There was plenty of material to hand for the opposition. The administrative scandals, the trials of high officials, and above all a number of serious rebellions[1] which broke out about this time gave ample illustra-

[1] These were the rebellions of the Hereros and the Bondelzwarts in South West Africa, of the Bane Bule and the Batchengos in Kamerun, and of the Wahehe in East Africa.

tion of the justice of their case. Led by Erzberger, Roeren, and Bebel, the opposition

'reduced to absurdity the claim that "the German flag carrying the Cross and Kultur was winning the African continent for civilisation and Christianity". They exposed in no unrestrained language the oppression, even enslavement of the natives, and the manner in which they were swindled and exploited by the traders who brought in the *Schnaps* and *Putzwaren*; the robbing of their lands and cattle by the big companies; and the cruelty of the forced labour on the plantations, in the mines and on the public works. These critics held up to ridicule, as shining examples of German and Christian "Kulturträger", such men as Peters, Wehlan, Puttkamer, Arenberg, Leist and Wegner, who had used their official positions to further their own ambitions, to give play to their own licentious passions, and with whose "scandals" the press and the country had rung for many years past'.[1]

They attacked especially the economic exploitation of the colonies by the big capitalist companies and the political corruption to which they resorted to secure their advantages. Although the colonies belonged to Germany, they pointed out that the German people derived no benefit from them, but, on the contrary, had to pay large sums each year to subsidize an inefficient administration.

The parliamentary struggle came to a head in 1906. In the election of that year the Government, thanks to the desertion of the *Freisinnige Partei* and its own

[1] Townsend, op. cit., p. 234.

unparalleled electioneering activity, defeated the Opposition. But the agitation had achieved its purpose and the whole system of colonial administration was overhauled. This constructive period is associated with the name of Bernhard Dernburg, a man of great ability and integrity. In 1907 the Colonial Office, under his direction, became autonomous. He had already had experience of colonial problems as Governor of New Guinea; he supplemented this by visits to Africa, to the British Colonial Office, and to the U.S.A., in order to study cotton culture. In the colonies finances were reorganized, the law-codes brought into closer relation with native custom, and the administration reconstituted. Specialized training of officials was insisted upon and thoroughly carried out. Dernburg was eager to introduce some form of representative government: he extended the system of colonial legislative councils and inculcated a new attitude towards the native and his rights. Most important of all, he took in hand the work of economic development, broke with the *damnosa hereditas* of the concession system, and began the process of redeeming lands and grants already given away. Although Dernburg did much to educate German opinion to a sense of its responsibilities, he was faced with violent opposition from the colonial settlers and planters, whose hostility mainly contributed to his fall in 1910.

Dernburg's successors, Dr. Lindequist and Dr. Solf, however, carried on his work, and by 1914 the fruits of his efforts were just beginning to appear. The production of the colonies had been materially increased, great work had been done in medical and agricultural science, education and the improvement of communications had been steadily pushed forward. By 1913 there were 4,000 missionary schools and 100 government schools in the German colonial empire, with over 186,000 pupils. In 1901 the famous Institute for Tropical Diseases was founded in Hamburg; fine contributions to medical knowledge were made by Dr. Krueger and Dr. Kütz in dealing with small pox, and by Robert Koch, who faced and solved the problems of sleeping sickness. Indeed, from 1906 to 1914 the Germans can claim to have made a notable advance upon the attitude of the previous twenty years.

Dr. Townsend's conclusion, after a detailed study of German colonial policy, may be quoted at length:

'During the first twenty years of Germany's colonial history,' she writes, 'the native had been most cruelly treated and unjustly exploited. In short, he had suffered the same fate as befalls any such population throughout those stormy initial years which lay the foundations of all colonial empires. Robbed of his lands, his home, his freedom, and often wantonly and cruelly of his life, by the colonial adventurer, official or trading company, his continuous and fierce revolts were but tragic witnesses to his wretchedness and helplessness. Nothing, indeed, is more significant of the change for the better in the attitude of Germany's colonial administration toward the native than the fact that there occurred no actual native uprisings during the years 1908–1914. Peace prevailed throughout the overseas empire. And, freed from the

Political Arguments

burden of prosecuting an almost constant and devastating warfare in the colonies, the Colonial Office could direct its energies and resources towards a constructive rather than a destructive rule' (p. 273).

The emphasis which was laid by the Allied Powers upon Germany's moral unfitness to possess colonies was, despite the record of her government up to 1906, disproportionate. The Allied statesmen, while they derived most of their information about misgovernment from the campaign of the German opposition parties in 1904–6, gave no credit for the vigorous and honest attempts then made by the Germans themselves to remedy conditions, nor to the success attained by the new policy of Bernhard Dernburg. The Colonial Office after 1907 strove hard to correct the mistakes of the earlier period. The land laws of 1895 in East Africa and of 1896 in Kamerun—reinforced in 1907 and 1910—were belated but sincere attempts to control the purchases of native land by white settlers and to secure adequate reserves for the natives. After 1907, despite violent opposition, forced labour was made legal only for public works, and even then had to be paid. Nor can the charge of militarization be fairly brought against Germany. In 1914 there were in the German colonies 7,000 troops and police in all, an inadequate force even to defend their own territories. It is the French who are much more open to this charge. No colonial troops were used by Germany in Europe, but the French employed great numbers of Africans on the Western Front, and after the War in the Ruhr and Rhineland, and they have subsequently introduced militarization into their mandated territories in flat contradiction to Article 22 of the Covenant.

The 'Colonial Guilt lie' was also unnecessary to the real strength of the Allies' position in 1919. Mr. L. S. Amery has written: 'As for Germany's moral unfitness to govern natives (which did not, of course, figure in the actual treaty) that was of a piece with much else that was said, in speeches and even official correspondence, that belonged to the not wholly dispassionate atmosphere of the time. But it was essentially incidental, and added nothing to the real reasons for the Allied decision', which, he declares, was based on strategical grounds, and on the 'evidence that, even before the War, Germany had looked towards an expansion of her African Empire as the result of a successful war against ourselves'.[1] Mr. Lloyd George corroborates Mr. Amery's statement.[2]

The real motives of the Allies, and the relation of those motives to the Fourteen Points and to general international considerations in 1919, have been previously discussed (*ante*, chap. II).

Few people would wish to-day to perpetuate the accusation of 'colonial guilt'. But to say this is by no means to agree to the German demand for the return of their former colonies. On the contrary, to place the

---

[1] Quoted from *Journal of Royal African Society* (1937) in 'Germany's Claim to Colonies', p. 56.

[2] *The Truth about the Peace Treaties*, i, pp. 114–31.

question of 'colonial guilt' in its right proportion has the effect, not of destroying the case for the action which the Allies took at Versailles, but of strengthening it. Moreover, the fact that German colonial administration from 1906 to 1914 showed marked improvement over the preceding period affords no reason for believing that the same progress would be continued to-day. There is indeed ground for fearing that a Nazi colonial régime is much more likely to approximate to the conditions of the period before 1906. The reforms of 1906-14 were very largely due to pressure exerted upon the Government by public opinion, especially by the violent criticisms of the Socialist leaders in the Reichstag. In the Germany of to-day, where freedom of speech, freedom of the press, and the Liberal and Socialist parties are all suppressed, such guarantees of good government as are afforded by criticism no longer exist. In 1926 Dr. Heinrich Schnee's book on German Colonization was translated into English by Mr. W. H. Dawson. Mr. Dawson looked with favour upon the proposal to return her former colonies to Germany; yet it is interesting to find that even so convinced a partisan of the German cause founded his support upon 'the confident belief that to-day, when the German people for the first time in its history is in effective control of national policy and affairs, these territories and peoples could count, under the care of their earlier and rightful trustees, on just, clement and sympathetic treatment' (p. 19). Mr. Dawson asserts that the evils of the earlier period of German colonial rule were largely due to the militarist character of the Government: he assumes that Germany is freed for ever from such control and that she will remain a democratic country. In 1926, upon Mr. Dawson's assumptions, many—though not all—of the members of this Group would have felt inclined to agree with him and to support the return of her colonies to Germany as a just and expedient course of action. To-day, with those assumptions proved false, most of us feel considerable doubt whether the interests of either justice or expediency will be best served in this way.

III

From the discussions of the Group it was evident that there was a difference of opinion upon the difficult and controversial subject of native policy. Widely divergent views were, in consequence, expressed as to the probable effect on the natives of their being restored to German rule. It seems to the editors that there is no satisfactory alternative to an impartial description of these differences of opinion.[1]

One section of the group accepted the attitude to native policy which is usually ascribed to the Government of the Union of South Africa and to General Smuts. In this view, the future civilization of Africa

[1] On the whole question of native policy see: L. P. Mair, *Native Policies in Africa* (London, 1936); E. H. Brookes, *The Colour Problems of South Africa* (London, 1934); W. M. Macmillan, *The Cape Colour Question* (London, 1927), and *Africa Emergent* (London, 1938); I. L. Evans, *Native Policy in Southern Africa* (Cambridge, 1934); Leonard Barnes, *Caliban in Africa* (London, 1930).

Political Arguments

depends upon the establishment of a large and prosperous white community on that continent, which will propagate and exemplify the highest achievements of European civilization. This object can only be achieved if the black and white races are kept rigidly apart. Only by this means can European standards be prevented from deteriorating as the result of contact with the numerically superior black race. Only by this means, too, can the native be protected from the injuries which will otherwise be inflicted on him by the impact of white civilization. This policy of segregation, however, is applied completely only in the social and political field. In the economic field the co-operation of native labour is regarded as necessary to the full development of white civilization, the *sine qua non* of progress for every inhabitant of Africa. For the same reason it is regarded as necessary to take every precaution to protect the white wage-earner from the competition of cheap native labour. The natives should therefore be confined to the performance of unskilled tasks.

Other views were expressed, however, which agreed in rejecting any solution of the problem which appeared to relegate native interests to an immediately subordinate position, and which were frankly critical of the South African policy. They agreed, too, in regarding a composite civilization to which both African and Europeans elements would contribute as the object of sound native policy. There was some divergence of view, however, as to the methods by which this object would be achieved. By some great stress was laid on the necessity of concentrating principally on the preservation of African society and on the avoidance of the assumption that the Africa of the future would necessarily be dominated rather by European than by African ideals. For this reason it was considered to be of vital importance that nothing should be done to imperil existing native society. Above all it should be preserved from the disintegrating influences which would necessarily follow from the intensive economic exploitation of native areas by European methods, and to a lesser degree from any considerable extension of white settlement. Progress there would be, but it would be progress strictly regulated by the capacity of native society to absorb the achievements of European experience without losing its own identity. The form of civilization which would emerge from this process was not regarded as being a question of immediate moment. But it was considered that any policy which ignored the fact 'that African institutions have a definite value for the peoples who have evolved them' was bound to be disastrous.[1]

This view takes very seriously the idea of trusteeship, of which so much has been heard since the War. The classic enunciation of trusteeship was made in the White Paper of 1923, which laid down the principles of the Government's policy in Kenya:

'Primarily Kenya is an African territory and H.M.'s Government think it necessary definitely to record their

[1] See Mair, op. cit., chapter vii.

Political Arguments

considered opinion that the interests of the African natives must be paramount, and that if, and when, those interests and the interests of the immigrant races should conflict, the former should prevail.'

The most striking experiments in 'trusteeship' have been carried out in Nigeria and Tanganyika, where Lord Lugard and Sir Donald Cameron have introduced the system known as 'indirect rule'. Adopted first as an expedient for

'dealing with an unmanageable administrative problem in a large and populous country, it developed into a philosophy of native administration directed towards the education of primitive peoples for the orderly control of their own affairs, without too suddenly importing European ideas; towards the fostering of native institutions with the definite purpose of providing a civilisation not alien, but having its roots in the past; and towards building on the foundations of those institutions a real administrative and financial local autonomy. Native social practice and judicial procedure are by careful guidance gradually to be brought into agreement with Western conceptions, instead of being replaced by alien institutions imperfectly understood. In this way native societies may become active units of local government and the native social organisation, with its restraints, will be maintained. Indirect rule is intended, in Lord Lugard's words, "to promote the evolution and adaptation of native institutions as opposed to Europeanisation and assimilation"',[1]

and also, we may add, to a policy of segregation and the pre-eminence of the white community.[2]

[1] *The Colonial Problem*, p. 258.
[2] Reference may be made to the following: A. D. A. de Kat

Other members of the group were less inclined to stress the necessity of slow and cautious progress and more confident of the universal validity of European civilized ideals. While not denying the necessity of taking into account the existing peculiarities of native society, they were less confident that they had any permanent contribution to make to a common civilization. 'Our own history, if it teaches anything, bears witness on every page how much human development—one had once dared to say "progress"—has been due precisely to that "clash of cultures" which now gives rise to anxious solicitude.'[1] They insisted on the danger of the policy of 'indirect rule' becoming synonymous with the preservation of the meaningless or harmful characteristics of a primitive tribal society.

It is a matter of some dispute whether the present policy of the British Government in Nigeria and Tanganyika is more in harmony with the first or second of these views. But it is at least sufficiently clear that it stands in sharp antithesis to the practice of the Union Government, and to the policy which the German Government, with its insistence on the necessity of rapid economic exploitation, would be likely to follow. The return of her former African

---

Angelino, *Colonial Policy* (Eng. trans. The Hague, 1931); Cameron, *Principles of Native Administration and their Application* (Lagos, 1935); Margery Perham, *Native Administration in Nigeria* (Oxford, 1937); Buell, *The Native Problem in Africa* (New York, 1928); Shapero, *Western Civilisation and the Natives of South Africa*.

[1] W. M. Macmillan, *Africa Emergent*, p. 378.

colonies to Germany could only mean the complete reversal of the present policy. To quote Lord Lugard's own words:

'The British policy of trusteeship—however sceptical some nations may be about its altruism, and in spite of some failures—is a very real thing which no British stateman dare ignore. . . . It is the declared policy of H.M.'s Government to train the natives to "stand alone" at some distant time, and to give them as much share in the government as they are from time to time capable of. This policy has been rejected by Herr Hitler and in consequence it adds to the reasons for British refusal to transfer even Mandates to Germany.'[1]

Even if the Germans maintained the highest standards of justice and administration, it was pointed out by members of the Group that the success of a colonial policy lies in something more subtle and more fundamental than material benefits for the native peoples, or the cold, impartial dispensation of justice; that it lies in the personal relationships of blacks and whites, in the reaction of the whites to colour and primitiveness, in the impalpable atmosphere of sympathy and understanding. The record of the Nazi Government, its colonial inexperience, its emphasis upon racial superiority, its pressing economic needs, do not lead one to suppose that it would be successful in meeting these wider demands.

It has not been sufficiently realized how great a change transfer would mean for the native

[1] Quoted in *Germany's Claim to Colonies*, p. 52.

communities. Mr. Harold Nicolson did not exaggerate when he wrote:

> 'Colonies are not static pieces of territory, they are living organisms in process of rapid development. To surrender them would not entail merely the signature of some deed of gift; it would entail a major surgical operation. By such transfer we should be breaking pledges and disappointing serious hopes.'[1]

The difficulties of adjustment for a primitive people are great enough: transfer to another administration would only heighten their emotional tragedy. The use of a different language and of a different currency offer two examples of such difficulties. But we must go farther than this. It is becoming increasingly clear that the differences between English and German civilization go far deeper than questions of language and currency. In the imponderable values which are the genius of a civilization we differ radically. The relationship of the individual to the state, our moral and religious ideas, the pattern of our social relations —all these are different. If Germany re-enters Africa she brings Nazism and its whole philosophy with her. For the native the change would be revolutionary and the strain of adjustment perhaps too great. This argument does not apply with equal force to all the former German possessions; it applies far less to South West Africa—under Union government and policy—than to Tanganyika and the Cameroons, but it is a very powerful argument against the return of the latter.

[1] Quoted in *Germany's Claim to Colonies*, p. 53.

Political Arguments

The German spokesmen have made it clear that they would not consider the return of their ex-colonies under mandatory limitations. Thus General von Epp in 1935 stated that 'Germany has no interest in Mandates, but demands for her own that which rightly belongs to her before God and man'.[1] We have to recognize, therefore, that return means the loss of all that has been gained by the Mandates system, which, though admittedly imperfect, still represents, in its guarantees for good government, an advance upon previous colonial administration.

General von Epp has also indignantly denied that German racial legislation would operate to hurt the natives' interests. In the *Europaïsche Revue* for September 1936 he wrote:

'It is a contradiction in terms to pretend, as has often been done recently, that, owing to the racial legislation at home, Germany has proved herself incapable of educating alien races and administering their wealth. It is the characteristic of Germany's racial legislation precisely to respect and encourage, as well as to assist, the development of the qualities of those races which differ from her own. Germany has no intention of interfering with the racial affairs of native peoples. We are simply anxious to prevent the intrusion of foreign racial elements into our population, and this on racial grounds. Those who think this is a reason for denying Germany's capacity to govern native peoples ought rather to examine the history of many another nation which boasts of its talent for colonising.'[2]

[1] Ibid., p. 30. [2] Ibid., p. 33.

The General may be right, but it is not an argument that will be accepted with much conviction outside Germany. Nothing is so likely to lead to disregard of native interests and abuse of power as a policy of swift economic exploitation, and the Germans have made no secret of their intention to exploit the material resources of the colonies as rapidly and as thoroughly as possible. All the long experience of colonization goes to show that this policy must prove disastrous to the native. The tragic record of the wrongs inflicted upon the native in the name of economic development is long enough. Must we return to a stage of civilization from which at last there appears to be hope of escaping?

Nor can we exclude the possibility that Germany's return to Africa would mean the extension of the European arms race to Africa. The effects of the Italian policy of militarization in North Africa are already becoming apparent. For the native populations these effects are wholly bad: they create a restless frame of mind, destroy the traditional pattern of life, and retard the process of development. Every administrator has borne witness to the evil consequences of the Great War in this respect. The prospect of native conscription for the purpose of supplying not only the economic but also the military needs of the European Powers is one from which we may well revolt in horror.

Although there was not complete unanimity in the Group upon all the issues which we have raised in this

Political Arguments

section, there was substantial agreement upon the conclusion that, from the colonial and the native point of view, the return of her former colonies to Germany is undesirable. This being so, it appears to be incompatible with conscience or responsibility to suggest the bartering of colonies and populations in the alleged interests of a European settlement, when, by such action, the destinies of millions of human beings will be changed, and changed perhaps for the worse.

IV

It is clear that the colonial issue is not the affair of England and Germany alone. It is part of a general world situation which concerns, either immediately or indirectly, every Power and people. Viewed from that angle, its problems are many and intricate; but in a kaleidoscopic political scene they must remain largely speculative until the colonial question has reached the stage of 'joinder of issue'. The wider international considerations lie beyond the scope of this book, since the object of the Group's discussions was to examine those objective factors of the colonial problem which seemed to be at least approximately calculable. We therefore content ourselves with a very brief reference to certain of the more general implications which arose incidentally in discussion, and which have been so much canvassed in the press and elsewhere that they need no elaboration here.

It has frequently been urged that the colonial

question cannot and must not be treated as a separate issue, but only as part of an 'all-round settlement' which, by clearing up the outstanding questions of Versailles, as between the 'satisfied' and the 'dissatisfied' nations, will give Europe a new start. The late Lord Allen of Hurtwood, a prominent advocate of this view, has put it thus:

'There is only one way in which the colonial question can be dealt with at this stage, and that is as part of an all-round settlement in which there is give and take on both sides and in which our German friends not only receive a reconsideration of that problem, but themselves contribute to the necessary security which we need if there is to be a peace settlement for Europe.'[1]

While recognizing the force of this contention, the Group did not feel that it could be profitably discussed until the nature of the proposed 'all-round settlement' was more exactly defined. It is not known at present whether the German Government would even be prepared to consider the question from an 'all-round' point of view, or would prefer to make a peremptory demand for the return of what it declares to be merely stolen property. All that can be said is that nothing in Herr Hitler's utterances up to the present time indicates the least inclination to any form of compromise.

Some members of the Group maintained that it had been too lightly assumed that 'appeasement' was the sole object to which every sacrifice, including the 'all-

[1] Quoted in *Germany's Claim to Colonies*, p. 57.

Political Arguments

round settlement', should be made. What became (it was asked) of the interests of the natives? If it was true that transfer of territory would be at the expense of the native populations, should we wholly disregard that fact for the sake even of a better Europe? Against this, it was urged that reconciliation between the Great Powers, by providing the opportunity for peaceful development throughout the whole world, would, in the long run, enure to the benefit of primitive peoples no less than of civilized nations.

A question not dissimilar to the last arises from the purely British point of view. What guarantee has Great Britain of any reciprocity in a colonial settlement with Germany? England is asked to return colonies which came to her, as most colonial possessions have come to powerful nations, by victory in war; apart from loss of territory and wealth, she would expose herself to certain strategic dangers which are discussed elsewhere in this book. Is she to be expected to impose this self-denying ordinance without receiving either guarantees or compensation? If not, what guarantees or compensation has Germany ever suggested? Members of the Group were unable to find any parallel in history for a return, in this unqualified manner, of colonies acquired after a long and desperate struggle—colonies which, for nearly a generation, the tutelary Power has conscientiously done her best to administer according to enlightened modern notions of colonial government.

Another view, which has often been advanced—

most explicitly, perhaps, by Mr. Harold Nicolson[1]—is that the German demand for colonies is only partly sincere, and is exploited chiefly as a bargaining instrument, or, as it is sometimes expressed, for the sake of its 'nuisance-value'. It is, according to this view, only a kind of feint to provide a diversion while the main attack is delivered in eastern Europe—in short, a mere manœuvre in the policy of the 'free hand'. Those who hold this opinion point to the comparatively small place which colonial expansion occupies in the ambitions of *Mein Kampf*, and consider it not without significance that at Godesberg, while Herr Hitler singled out the colonial question as an outstanding issue between England and Germany, he expressly deprecated the notion that it could amount to a *casus belli*.[2] It is clear that, if the colonial demand is intended to be merely a distraction from a more serious engagement, the whole of the present discussion is academic. This question, however, must necessarily remain hypothetical until Germany has explained herself more fully or has made definite proposals.

In many minds, perhaps the most anxious doubt of all is whether a sacrifice by England, made for the sake of general settlement, would really achieve its object. It is unnecessary to do more here than to refer to the various forms in which this scepticism has

[1] See 'The Colonial Problem', *International Affairs*, January–February 1938, p. 40.

[2] The statement was reaffirmed in Herr Hitler's Reichstag speech of 30 Jan. 1939.

expressed itself. Would Germany, now so vociferously 'dissatisfied', be contented by concession upon a single issue—or would the appetite grow by what it fed on? Even if her intentions were sincere and conciliatory, would she not soon be disappointed with her prize? Has she not greatly exaggerated the value of her former colonies, and would she not again become aggrieved when she found that colonies did not yield the economic relief which she expected, or professed to expect—fallaciously, as has been here suggested, since the root of her economic difficulties lies in a constricted world trade and in her own self-sufficiency experiment? Above all, would any concession in the colonial field make the least difference to Germany's aspirations in Europe itself? Have not those aspirations been proclaimed beyond any possibility of doubt in *Mein Kampf*—are they not accepted as gospel by official Nazi opinion, and would a few overseas possessions, which might perhaps turn out to be more a liability than an asset, convert these aggressive doctrines into the policy of the 'good neighbour'? Again, from a more technical point of view, which perhaps is merely pedantic to Germany but certainly cannot be ignored by England, what is the position of the League of Nations in the whole matter? Whereas England is bound to respect the status of the League in any question concerning Mandates, is Germany, in her present mood, likely to accord the League any *locus standi* whatever in a dispute which she appears to regard as purely her own affair? Finally, is there not reason for thinking that it is part of the technique of the present régime in Germany to exacerbate rather than mollify a sense of grievance and constantly to create new demands for the redress of wrongs, so as to be able to produce, in an emotional atmosphere, a swelling record of successes, 'vindications', and 'rights' wrested, in the name of justice, from snarling dogs in the manger?

Each individual will answer these questions according to his own interpretation of past and future tendencies in German policy; but the very existence of such doubts and suspicions, which are widely felt and which are both resented and recriminated by Germany, are, we feel, a formidable stumbling-block on the threshold. On the one hand, it is only fair to recognize that, to German eyes, it seems like a disparaging prejudgement, which in effect destroys all basis of negotiation, to say at the outset: 'We cannot give you an inch, because it will only encourage you to take an ell.' On the other hand, it is a perfectly reasonable method of bargaining, and indeed a measure of common prudence, to form a pre-estimate of the good faith of the other party on the evidence of his past actions, methods, and professions. It is not within our purpose or capacity to suggest a counsel of perfection in this dilemma; what seems certain to us is that any proposal for return of the colonies, even if couched as an invitation to negotiate and not as a brusque demand, would be launched under unfavourable auspices unless there were a far more solid basis

Political Arguments

of mutual confidence than exists at present, or seems likely to exist, between totalitarian and democratic Powers.

V

It is necessary to realize the effects which colonial concessions might have upon the future existence of the British Empire. In this last section we propose to consider these effects.

The first and most obvious is the increased difficulty of imperial defence. A glance at the map will show that the possession of the former German colonies by a hostile power would constitute a serious threat to two, possibly three, of the main trade-routes of Great Britain. From Asia and from Australasia in 1937 we drew 26 per cent. of our imports. This trade must come by one of two routes, either through the Suez Canal or round the Cape: the Pacific route is too long to be used except for a small proportion of goods. Ships coming either by the Suez Canal or by the Cape route must cross the Indian Ocean and could be hampered by raiders, especially submarines, operating from bases in Tanganyika. Shipping by the Cape route would also have to pass close by South West Africa and within striking distance of raiders from the Cameroons, who might also trouble the important trade-route from South Africa converging on the West African coast. In time of war, in view of the insecurity of our Mediterranean communications, the Cape route will become of first-rate importance, and we cannot afford to add to the difficulties of its protection. Those who belittle the importance of such strategic arguments point to the superiority of the British over the German Navy; they forget, however, to add that the British Navy will have to be scattered over the whole world to protect our commitments and that the strength of the Italian and German submarine fleets in proportion to their total naval tonnage is very high —a significant fact. Sir Samuel Hoare put the question very neatly when he said: 'If our sea communications are cut, we have a supply of raw materials that will only last our industries for 3 months, but that supply would be more than we need, for within 6 weeks we should be dead by starvation.' German use of her former colonies as naval bases would certainly not mean the cutting of our sea communications; but there is no need gratuitously to increase our difficulties, which are already very considerable.

The military, as well as the naval, position would also be affected by return. In Africa, German possession of South West Africa would bring the principal towns of the Union within range of aerial bombardment. Tanganyika is no less important. It is a vital link in communications between North and South Africa both by land and by air; its loss would mean the breaking of the Cape–Cairo line and the increased isolation of South Africa. Two other possibilities have to be considered. Would German-Italian co-operation continue in Africa? If it did, we might well have to face the prospect of Kenya and Uganda being caught between a German Tanganyika and an Italian Abyssinia and Somaliland. During the Great War much was also heard of another German plan for expansion in Africa, the famous Mittel-Afrika dream of Emil Zimmermann and his followers. It is not impossible that such a scheme might be revived on the same grandiose scale as the new Roman Empire of Fascist Italy, if her former colonies were returned to Germany outside the framework of a successful general settlement.

In the Pacific, Australia looks upon New Guinea in much the same way as the Union looks upon South West Africa: she regards its possession as vital to her defence. Naval and aerial bases in New Guinea in the possession of a power hostile to the British Empire and friendly to Japan would cause deep concern in Australia. It is not Germany that is regarded as the danger in the Far East, but Japan. Japan lacks any forward base at present for operations against Australia or the immensely valuable East Indies. It is not, however, altogether outside the bounds of probability, in view of the anti-Comintern Pact, that Japan might find German bases in New Guinea available for her use. Australia, at all events, is not inclined to take the risk.

The effects of return upon the British Empire can, however, by no means be limited to the sphere of imperial defence. The Dominions have, from the very first, taken a strong line about the territories which they now administer under mandate. In 1919 it was the Dominions Prime Ministers who wanted annexation, and since that date they have frequently reaffirmed their determination to keep what they already have. A decision on the part of the British Government in favour of return might well meet with determined opposition within the Empire. A situation might thereby arise in which certain sections of opinion within the Dominions would raise a demand for withdrawal from the Empire. One of the most cogent arguments for the continued association of the Dominions with the Empire is their need for British help to defend their interests. Should Great Britain fail to meet that need, the whole force of the argument would be destroyed. A policy of return could only be advocated by the British Government at a grave risk of destroying imperial solidarity.

The repercussions of such action would be felt as well in the Colonial empire as in the Dominions. All Africans who have any knowledge of international events have been gravely disturbed by the fate of Abyssinia and by the failure of Great Britain and the other League Powers to check the Italian aggression. The African native is far from being a fool: if he sees Great Britain hand over the native populations of Tanganyika or the Cameroons to Germany, he will conclude that trusteeship and concern for the interests of the natives are no more than empty phrases and that, when it suits the convenience of his rulers, he and his land will be bartered about, without the least regard for his rights or feelings as an individual.

Whatever sentiment of trust and respect now exists for British rule in Africa would be seriously undermined by action which less subtle minds might feel tempted to describe as betrayal.

PART II

V

SOUTH WEST AFRICA

I

THE vast territory of South West Africa, which stretches from the northern banks of the Orange River to the southern frontier of Angola, was the first acquisition of the German colonial empire. The nucleus of the colony was Angra Pequena Bay, where a German merchant, Lüderitz, established a 'factory' in 1883 and secured concessions of land and trading rights from the local chiefs. Although Great Britain had several times refused to extend British sovereignty beyond Whale Bay in the north, the Government was disturbed and irritated by Bismarck's announcement in April 1884 that Lüderitz's settlement was under the protection of the German Empire. The Cape Government was much more alarmed and inclined even to combat the German claims. Mr. Gladstone's Government, however, had suffered more than enough from colonial entanglements and on 22 September 1884 accepted the *fait accompli*, admitting the German claim to sovereignty over the whole coast from the Orange River to the frontier of Angola. The next year the Cape Government reconciled itself to the situation, and a joint commission, which met at Capetown, fixed the future frontiers of the territory to the general satisfaction.

The colony from the first fell far short of German expectations. Much of the country proved to be waterless desert; long droughts and an epidemic of rinderpest in 1897 aggravated the natural difficulties of developing the land; and, most important of all, the relations between the Germans and their native subjects remained uneasy.

In 1893-4 a partial rising of the Hereros and Hottentots under the chief Hendrik Witbooi had been suppressed by Major Leutwein. The outbreak of rinderpest in 1897 led to further disorders; but these Leutwein was again successful in quelling without great difficulty, thanks to the loyal support of Hendrik Witbooi. The spirit of revolt, however, still persisted and the behaviour of the German colonists did not make the situation easier. Against the natives, who were dependent upon them for all the goods they needed, the traders enforced their claims for payment in a callous and oppressive manner. If the money could not be obtained by threats, the natives' cattle, their stock, and land were confiscated, and even the tribes' possessions were distrained upon when the individual's resources were insufficient.

The grievance most deeply felt related to the land, of which the natives were being rapidly and unfairly dispossessed. Leutwein himself quotes from one of the native petitions addressed to him as Governor:[1]

'We notice with dismay', the petition runs, 'that our lands pass one after another into the hands of the whites,

[1] Leutwein, *Elf Jahre Gouverneur in Deutsch-Südwestafrika*.

and in consequence we humbly pray Your Excellency not to authorize any sale of land here, and to transfer all the lands which have not yet been sold into a great reserve, for we should then be certain, we and our children, that we should have a territory where we could live and cultivate our farms.'

Leutwein, indeed, did what he could to control the sale of lands and to set aside adequate reserves for the natives. In 1898 he also issued regulations limiting the time during which commercial debts could be recovered, a measure which was reinforced by a revised code, issued by the German Colonial Council.

These measures were certainly steps in the right direction, but they were carried only in the face of bitter hostility from the colonists, who, by their refusal to co-operate with the Administration, were largely successful in preventing their enforcement. The Hereros, at all events, reached the conclusion that further reliance upon the Government was useless, and late in 1903 they revolted, together with the Hottentots of the south, under Hendrik Witbooi.

The situation which gave rise to the Herero rebellion is in itself a serious reflection upon the German administration. But the manner in which that rebellion was suppressed goes far to justify the most severe judgements upon the character of German colonial rule before 1906. In June 1904 General von Trotha was sent out to take command. The notorious proclamation of 20 October 1904 gave an indication of the policy he intended to pursue.

South West Africa

'The Herero people must now leave the country; if they do not, I will compel them to go. Within the German frontier every Herero, with or without a rifle, with or without cattle, will be shot. I will not take over any men, women, or children, but I will either drive them back to your people or have them fired on.'

In a military sense von Trotha's policy proved successful: the revolt was crushed. Many of the Herero who escaped from the Germans perished of thirst and starvation in the Kalahari Desert; those who were caught were shot or hanged out of hand. On his return, von Trotha had to face a storm of criticism in Germany. The Government justified his actions and gave him official protection, but the force of public opinion could not be ignored and the proclamation was withdrawn. Indeed, from any other point of view than the military von Trotha's policy was disastrous. In 1898 the native population was estimated by Governor Leutwein at 300,000: in 1912 it totalled only a third of that number. Those Herero who survived were pressed into service and forbidden to own cattle, a severe punishment for a pastoral people, whose whole economy of life had been based upon the possession of cattle, and whose deepest feelings were outraged by the seizure and slaughter of their sacred herds.

Dr. Paul Rohrbach summed up the situation with candour when he wrote:

'The land question is solved, for the Hereros have lost their land, which is now fiscal property, and is settled by whites. The cattle question is also solved, for the whole of the live stock of the Hereros has been destroyed: there are hardly any cattle left.'[1]

From their treatment at the hands of the Germans, the Herero people, formerly one of the great Bantu tribes of southern Africa, have never recovered. The Report of the Judicial Commission of the Union Government in 1936 bore witness to the miserable and degraded existence which the remnant of the tribe now lead, thirty years after the suppression of the revolt. Such is the legacy of von Trotha's policy of 'thorough'.

After the suppression of the rebellion the economic resources of the territory were more effectively developed: the herds of cattle, of sheep, and of goats steadily increased in numbers and the mineral wealth of the country was exploited under much stricter control after the Imperial Mining Ordinance of 1905. Nevertheless, the economic position of the country as a whole was unsound, and by 1913-14 South West Africa had a deficit of 38,520,000 marks, only 2,400,000 marks less than that of German East Africa, a far more densely populated country. Nor was the racial situation at all easy. The suppression of the Herero rebellion had created an atmosphere of hatred and distrust, and shortly before the War Dr. Karl Dove, a recognized authority upon South West Africa, could write:[2]

'The mass constitutes a permanent menace to security,

[1] Quoted in *German Colonisation* (F.O. Handbook, 1920), p. 123.
[2] Quoted ibid., p. 134, from *Deutsch-Südwestafrika*, p. 195.

South West Africa

because an ungovernable hatred of the whites lies in the hearts of these people, a hatred which no baptism of water will exorcise and no education eradicate so long as the rulers of the country continue to be whites.'

He advocated as a remedy the adoption of the 'Boer attitude towards the Kaffirs', with the interesting comment that 'leniency towards the blacks is cruelty to the whites'.

II

As a result of its conquest by South African troops during the War, South West Africa became a 'C' mandated territory under the administration of the Union. The Union Government has had to meet very grave difficulties in its conduct of the mandate and it is undeniable that since 1930 the situation in South West Africa has been far from satisfactory. We propose to make a brief survey of the main difficulties encountered, relying for our information upon two reports issued by the Union Government—that of the Commission on the Economic and Financial Relations of the Union and the Mandated Territory of South West Africa (1935) and that of the Judicial Commission of 1936.

The gravest obstacles to successful administration have been economic. These spring fundamentally from the nature of the country. A great deal of the land is desert. Along the entire Atlantic coast, to a depth of 50 to 90 miles, lies the Namib Desert, which, apart from the ports of Swakopmund, Walvis Bay, and Lüderitz, is practically uninhabited. The eastern parts of the territory are covered by the great Kalahari Desert. Conditions in the central area are better, and are suitable for cattle-ranching, but even here the comparative unproductiveness of the soil makes intensive settlement impossible. The size of the average farm is 32 sq. miles, yet even on this it is difficult for one family to support itself. The great and abiding difficulty is the lack of water. In the thirty years since 1900 there have been four long periods of drought—4 years, 1900–3; 2 years, 1915–16; 2 years, 1926–7; 5 years, 1929–33. Such water as can be obtained lies deep underground, and the cost of farming is greatly increased by the need to build elaborate pumping apparatus.

It is true that the territory has considerable mineral wealth, but Dr. W. P. de Kock, the director of mining in South West Africa up to 1935, told the Judicial Commission that the value of the mineral deposits had been exaggerated. While the beds of diamonds, copper, and other metals have yielded rich samples, they are widely dispersed and lacking in bulk. Moreover their exploitation involves great expense, which the mining companies lately have not been able to face.

The Mandatory Administration began with a clean slate financially in April 1920. It had no debts to encumber it and a balance of nearly a million pounds which had accrued during the military occupation. For the first ten years the financial situation was satisfactory: revenue exceeded expenditure and a good deal of capital development—the construction of docks at Walvis Bay and intensive land settlement—was undertaken. Since 1930, however, the situation has rapidly deteriorated. The public debt was estimated by the 1936 Commission at £3,671,900 (not including £524,000 paid by the Union Government for the settlement of the Angola Boers) and expenditure is still far in excess of revenue.[1]

The blame for this state of affairs has been laid in various quarters. In South West Africa itself there has been much criticism of the Union Government. It has been said that the policy of land settlement pursued by that Government was uneconomic and against the interests of the territory. The capital required by the settler is generally agreed to be about £2,500, yet the Union Government, it is argued, in its anxiety to settle its own nationals in South West Africa, has rarely demanded that the settler should have more than £250 capital. Up to 1932 over £1,300,000 had been spent in subsidizing settlers (an advance of about £2,035 per settler), and the inability of the settlers to repay these loans (well over £1 million is outstanding) has crippled the country's finances. A second grievance entertained against the Union Government is its loan policy. The debt per head of the white population was estimated by the 1936 Commission at £131 when that population numbered only 31,000. Out of a revenue of £669,140 in 1936, £183,253 had to be paid in debt redemption and interest. Such a policy

[1] In 1932 ordinary revenue was £357,388, ordinary expenditure £602,964.

must ultimately lead to the bankruptcy of the Administration: yet increased taxation offers little hope of a remedy, because so many of the inhabitants are already heavily in debt to the Government. Yet a third complaint against the Union is that the customs union of South West Africa and the Union works to the disadvantage of the former and that protection to the Union producer is given by differential freight rates on the railways. If this is true, it would be of great concern to South West Africa, which is commercially dependent upon South Africa.

The minority report of the Economic Commission (1935) believed that many of the charges against the Union were well founded, but the majority report could not accept this view. It ascribed the unsatisfactory condition of the territory to the continued drought from 1929 onwards which had ruined many farmers, to the world depression of the early thirties, and to the failure of the diamond mines to come up to expectations. The importance of this last point can be seen when it is realized that 60 per cent. of the profits from the mines are taken by the Government, and that revenue from this source declined from £310,085 in 1925–6 to £10,000 in 1932–3. The majority report inclined to exonerate the Union Government from many of the charges made against it, though it suggested that a modification of policy, especially in the matter of land settlement, was necessary.

These considerations, taken with the fact that in the last five years before the occupation the German

South West Africa

Imperial Exchequer contributed £679,000 per annum to the colony's finances, suggest that the economic arguments adduced by the Germans in support of their claim to colonies have no application at all to South West Africa. On the contrary, they show that the territory must remain a grave financial liability upon the resources of whatever country is responsible for its administration. The natural difficulties of development are so great that no policy, without subsidization, is likely to prove of much success. The fault is not that of the Union or its policy; circumstances, it appears, would prove too much for any Government. In particular, the failure of the settlement schemes in South West Africa, pursued with so much energy and enthusiasm in the twenties, shows conclusively the fallacy of the German argument that in her former colony she could find an outlet for her surplus population. If South African farmers, experienced in all the difficulties of African land development, have failed, there is very little reason to suppose that inexperienced European colonists would be more successful. While agreeing, therefore, that the present economic situation of South West Africa is unsatisfactory, we firmly believe that return to Germany would do nothing to meet the economic difficulties of either the territory itself or of Germany.

III

The political situation in South West Africa is similarly unsatisfactory. The Judicial Commission, in the

Report of 1936, unanimously agreed that 'the present form of government of the Territory is a failure and should be abolished'. Up to 1926 the country was governed by an Administrator appointed by the Union and assisted by an Advisory Council of nine. In that year new constitutional arrangements were adopted and since that time the Administrator has had, to help him, a Legislative Assembly consisting of twelve elected and six nominated members, and an Executive Committee of four members elected by the Assembly with the Administrator as Chairman. The powers of legislation possessed by the Assembly are limited. The following matters are reserved to the Union Government:

    (1) Native affairs,
    (2) Mineral exploitation,
    (3) Railways and harbours,
    (4) Civil service,
    (5) Courts of justice,
    (6) Communications,
    (7) Military affairs and service,
    (8) Immigration,
    (9) Tariffs,
    (10) Currency and banking.

The right to impose taxation is also reserved, except on the recommendation of the Administrator.

Two factors are responsible for the comparative failure of this limited form of representative government. The first is the economic and financial situation. Even the qualified independence of South West

Africa is seriously compromised by the heavy burden of public and private debt which lies upon practically the whole community. Many of the inhabitants, seriously disturbed at the financial prospect, feel that a radical alteration in the system of government is necessary. One of the most widely canvassed suggestions is that South West Africa should become a fifth province of the Union of South Africa. This was recommended in the 1936 Report by Mr. Justice van Zyl, who frankly stated his belief that the independence of South West Africa, in view of the financial and political situation, was an impracticable ideal. This view did not, however, command the support of his colleagues.

The second factor complicating the task of government is the problem of nationality. In 1914, at the end of the German occupation, there were about 13,000 German inhabitants in South West Africa. To-day, of the 31,000 Europeans, roughly 40 per cent. are of German descent. Relations between those of German stock and those who have immigrated from the Union have never been easy. They have become worse in recent years, first, because the Germans look upon the Union's policy of land settlement as a deliberate attempt to reduce them to the position of a racial minority, and secondly, because, with the advent of a nationalist Nazi Germany, they have become far more conscious of their racial distinctness and far less prepared to work amicably with the other inhabitants. The frequent attempts to achieve co-operation have all failed: the Germans are very impatient of a democratic form of government, and are bitterly hostile to the intervention of the Union and the suggestion that South West Africa should become a fifth province. Their demand is a frank one for return to Germany or at least increased independence from the Union's control. We shall examine the consequences of this attitude later: it is enough now to point to this very serious political and racial division in the community.

The success of native policy within the Mandated Territory varies considerably from tribe to tribe. The Union Government is directly responsible for the welfare of the natives and has not delegated these responsibilities to the South West African administration. The present state of the Herero and the Hottentots is far from satisfactory; yet, in fairness to the Union Government, it should be pointed out that the legacy of German policy towards the natives was so bad that any administration would have experienced great difficulty in raising the moral and physical condition of these tribes. With the Bondelzwarts, one of the smaller tribes, the Government had trouble in 1922–3, but, if one may judge by the Report of the Judicial Commission (1936), this tribe appears to be satisfied now with its treatment. It may also be pointed out that the advantages of some measure of international control (even in a C Mandate) were clearly demonstrated at the time of the Bondelzwart rising. The Permanent Mandates Commission

South West Africa

criticized the Union's policy strongly and by its intervention secured a just and successful solution of the dispute.

The majority of the native population, however, lives outside the Police Zone, removed from frequent contact with European communities. Roughly 165,000 of the 216,000 natives outside the Police Zone live in Ovamboland, a strip of territory in the extreme north, on the Angola frontier. Ovamboland holds a unique position in South West Africa. Even under German rule the operation of the local tribal organization was left practically untouched, and to-day it still serves as the basis of administration. Considerable judicial powers are exercised by the native courts, and the establishment of a Reserve Trust Fund, into which all taxes are paid, affords some measure of self-government. The responsibility for expenditure lies with the Native Commissioner, but he is assisted by a native council, six members of which are elected by the natives. In three of the tribes the chiefs, and in the other three the councils of headmen, are the recognized authorities.

The Judicial Commission of 1936 expressed considerable satisfaction with this experiment in indirect rule, but in other districts, e.g. the Okavango area, they found that there was still much to be done. They described the inhabitants as 'a low and degenerate type of native; they are a lazy and indolent people and lead a hand-to-mouth existence'.

Within the Police Zone, in regulating the relations

between natives and Europeans, parts of the Union's differential legislation have been adopted, including a master and servants law, a vagrancy law, and pass regulations. As Lord Hailey remarks,[1] however, the urgency of the situation in the Union is largely absent in South West Africa. More land is available for the native, there is no large 'poor white' community, and industrial activity plays a far smaller part in the life of South West Africa than in that of the Union. These factors may be expected to have a moderating influence upon the situation. Moreover, it should be pointed out that only one-third of the native population is to be found within the Police Zone and is affected by such legislation.

The Judicial Commission recommended no change in the general direction of native policy, though it made certain suggestions for the more efficient conduct of such a policy, such as increased medical services. But on the vexed question of the political future of the country as a whole no single solution was adopted by the different members of the Commission. Mr. Justice van Zyl favoured the inclusion of South West Africa within the Union of South Africa as a fifth province; Mr. J. van den Heever suggested the abolition of the present representative institutions, which have proved unworkable, and a return to a form of government comparable to that before 1926; Dr. J. E. Holloway believed that representative government should be eventually re-established,

[1] Hailey, *African Survey*, p. 374.

though he was prepared to accept an interim period during which administration should be in the hands of an Administrator with an Advisory Council. No agreement was reached by the Commission and three separate reports were presented upon the political problem.

The future policy of the Union towards South West Africa is not the direct concern of this report, but it is obviously of some importance, for if South West Africa is not to be included within the Union, or if no steps are likely to be taken to remedy what is admittedly an unsatisfactory position, there remains the possibility of return to Germany. For some years past the Germans have conducted in South West Africa a widespread campaign of propaganda and agitation which possesses all the characteristic features associated with the various Nazi drives in Central Europe.

The most reliable information of this agitation is to be found in the Report of the Judicial Commission for 1936, supplemented by later articles in the *Round Table*. The basis of Nazi activity in South West Africa is the exploitation of what is called dual nationality. Despite the fact that the great majority of the people of German race who reside in the territory are Union subjects, the German Government, as well as a certain section of the population of South West Africa, continue to regard all people of German race as the actual political subjects of the Reich. We are familiar with this idea in Europe and with the claims which Herr Hitler made, on this basis, to control the Sudeten

Deutsch and to interfere on their behalf, despite the fact that they were the legal subjects of another sovereign state. In South West Africa the position is even more complicated, because the exact nationality and status of the inhabitants of a mandated state is by no means clear. The inhabitants of South West Africa, a mandated state, are not subjects of the Union in the same full sense as, say, the inhabitants of Capetown, and the Germans have used this ambiguity to argue that all persons of German race, a great many of whom were former subjects of the German Empire, are still German subjects. Thus in a circular of December 1935, issued by the German party in South West Africa, the Deutsche Bund, it was asserted: 'German nationality is independent of naturalization and has not been lost by it. A person who has been a subject of the Reich remains a subject and has bequeathed that nationality to his children and grandchildren.'

The claims, which are put forward in direct contravention of the German-South African London Agreement of 1923, which attempted to solve the whole vexed question of 'dual nationality', are obviously capable of a sweeping application. As early as 1926 propaganda was being conducted for the return of the territory to Germany. And with the rise of the Nazi power since 1933 the campaign has been vastly intensified and the ambiguities of nationality widely exploited. In 1933 a certain Dr. Brenner was sent out, armed with funds and authority, to reorganize the existing Nazi party in South West Africa and to secure its domination over all other German organizations, including the official political party, the Deutsche Bund. He was but the first of a succession of such envoys. The campaign was directed from Germany by the *Auslandsabteilung* in Hamburg or by orders direct from Berlin and Munich. It included all the characteristic features of Nazi political drives. In 1934 an oath was generally administered: 'I swear that I will bear unbreakable allegiance to Adolf Hitler and yield unconditional obedience to leaders appointed by him over me.' Where individuals refused to take the oath reprisals were taken against their relatives in Germany. The oath was followed by the appointment of a Führer for South West Africa who directed the campaign to Nazify all the political, social, and cultural institutions of people of German race living within the territory. Propaganda was widely distributed and the German consul at Windhoek demanded that all history taught in the German schools should be upon a Nazi basis. A Nazi 'cell' organization was set up—*Stützpunkt*—and Hitler youth movements for all children, boys and girls, of German race were established. The object of the campaign, in the words of the local Führer, Weigel—an African Henlein—was 'to drum Hitler's programme into the Germans here, to make a fight for the return of South West Africa to Germany as soon as possible by calling every one a traitor and by treating as a traitor every one who does not think and act similarly. The territorial group keeps in touch with the authorities of the Homeland'.

The result was, as the 1936 Commission reported, that 'freedom of speech, of political association, and even of personal conduct has ceased to exist in the Territory for a large number of Germans who are Union subjects and who are entitled to the protection of the Mandatory'.

Following upon the Report of the Judicial Commission the Union issued a proclamation (December 1936) emphatically denying that it was considering the possibility of the transference of South West Africa to Germany. In October 1934 the official Nazi party had been dissolved; but Nazi activities were continued through the Deutsche Bund. On the activities of the Bund the Commission has reported unfavourably.

'The Bund as a whole', it said, 'is pledged to trim its policy according to directions received from Germany. There is no room for individual thought or action in the Bund. It has become a voting machine pledged to political and, at that, foreign dictation: the individual is dragooned into conformity by threats of reprisal and persecution. The situation has become impossible. It leaves no room for co-operation between the democratic Union section and the German element organized into a Nazi complex, which, through an ordered hierarchy, owes unquestioning obedience and allegiance to the head of a foreign state.'

The communiqué of December 1936, whilst declaring the Union's readiness to admit German as an official language in South West Africa and its willingness for the Germans to organize for the maintenance of their own cultural and social life, declared it henceforth illegal for aliens to be members of political organizations within the territory. This was consolidated in a proclamation of April 1937, which further made it an offence for any British subject to give allegiance to any other foreign state or its ruler. All non-British subjects engaged in political propaganda were to be deported under the same proclamation.

These measures brought hostile comment from the German press, as well as a note of protest from the German Government. The protest was rejected by General Hertzog, and despite the defiance of its leader, Herr Neuendorf, the Deutsche Bund was dissolved. Yet these measures do not appear to have been effective; Nazi activity continues. Thus in 1937 600 young Germans from the Territory, calling themselves the South West Africa National Group and vowing allegiance to Herr Hitler, were receiving training as political agitators and leaders in Germany before being sent back to South West Africa to continue the campaign. To-day in South West Africa the Nazi organization, though now secretly constituted, is no less complete and no less influential than it was before the dissolution of the Deutsche Bund. Its contacts with the German Government are still maintained, its purpose still adhered to, and the political situation is becoming more and more intolerable.[1]

[1] See Benjamin Bennett, *Hitler over Africa*, London, 1939.

The result of this situation upon the life of the Territory has been expressed by the 1936 Commission.

'It is common cause in South-West Africa that uncertainty as to the political future of the country is the basic reason for the dissatisfaction now prevalent. It retards the development of the country, makes investors of capital shy and has an unsettling effect on the inhabitants. The result is that they are inordinately preoccupied with politics; not the practical politics relating to the good government and advancement of the Territory, or touching upon their daily lives, but matters obscure and subtle, remote from use as far as their constitution is concerned, relating to world politics and the international situation.'

Apart from the German section of the population, which forms hardly more than two-fifths of the total European population of 31,600, opinion within South West Africa itself does not appear to favour the return of the colony to Germany. The opinion of the non-German Europeans is certainly divided on the question of inclusion within the Union; there are also complaints about the way in which the Mandate has been administered by the Union; but this does not mean that German annexation is therefore looked upon as a desirable alternative. The movement for return is confined to the people of German race.

The attitude of the natives is more difficult to assess, but this too would appear to be either hostile to return or indifferent. In no sense can there be said to be a pro-German movement among the natives. The Ovambo, the largest section of the native population, declared themselves in 1936 well satisfied with their position as Union subjects: in this territory interesting experiments are being made in indirect rule which are having considerable success. The Herero have certainly no wish to return to Germany after their disastrous experience of rebellion in 1904–7, when (as already noted) the tribe lost nearly half its population and suffered so severe a material and moral breaking that it has never recovered from it. Of the Herero and the other tribes, the Hottentots, the Damara, the Okavango, the Bastards, and the Bushmen, the 1936 Report speaks in disparaging tones; their material and moral condition is not good, but one must certainly not conclude from that fact that the natives are therefore in favour of return. On the contrary, they seem to have expressed themselves as either hostile or at most indifferent, through ignorance or depression.

Certainly in South West Africa a just conclusion would appear to be that no section of the population, black or white, except those of German race, favours a return to Germany or looks upon it as a desirable solution to South West Africa's difficulties. Whatever else the German Government may say, it cannot with truth represent the policy of return as one which would satisfy either the native population or a majority of the whites living in South West Africa.

Within the Union, apart from the small Nazi party, practically the whole of public opinion is united against transfer. The Government and the Dominion parties have publicly stated this. Dr. Malan, the leader of the National-Socialist party, tries to compromise by asserting that while Germany should have African territories, they should not be either South West Africa or Tanganyika. With this opinion certain sections of the United party are in agreement: their reason appears to be a belief that the Germans would take the same view of the colour question as they themselves do, and that their presence in Africa would thus strengthen that policy.

Those natives within the Union who have any knowledge of the matter are unanimously opposed to any territory in Africa being handed over to the Nazis. They have not yet forgotten the treatment of the Ethiopians by the Italians, and in recent crises the Bantu press has shown great indignation at the political and military policies of Germany, Italy, and Japan.

The intense German activity with regard to South West Africa naturally raises the question, Why does Germany desire its return? We have already recorded the opinion that the return of the former German colonies would not be a solution of Germany's economic problems. South West Africa is not a country which presents great economic possibilities, and even at the end of the German occupation the total number of German settlers was no more than 15,000. On the other hand, South West Africa has considerable strategic importance, which may—and in our view actually does—constitute its principal attraction to the new imperialist Germany.

South West Africa

This strategic importance is twofold: it affects Africa in particular and the British Empire in general. With regard to Africa, the possession of South West Africa was used by Germany before the War, and is desired by her now, as a foothold from which to spread her influence over a wider area. In other words, the possession of South West Africa is more important to Germany as a stepping-stone to the creation of a German empire in Africa than for its own sake. The Union must particularly feel itself threatened by German military power established upon its very borders. Before 1914 the Germans spent a good deal of money in constructing railways which could only be of use from a military point of view. As soon as war was declared in 1914 a rebellion occurred in the Union which had been carefully organized by the Germans from their forward base in South West Africa. The campaigns in South West Africa were undertaken by the Union simply because the Union could not feel itself safe with the hostile German power so near and able to make full use of any internal discontent within the Union. To return the territory to Germany would be simply to re-create that situation again and to reverse the military decision of 1914, with the added element that the danger would be heightened by the possibilities of air attack. There already exists a regular air service between Windhoek and Kimberley, a distance of no more than 600 miles. Capetown itself is only a bare 300 or 400 miles from the South West African border. To return South West Africa to Germany is therefore to destroy at one blow the protection of comparative isolation which the Union has hitherto enjoyed. Even if the danger can be met by an increase in armaments, that is in itself a serious financial problem for a state whose total income is only £39 millions, besides the perturbing possibilities which it creates of the use of native troops and their exploitation for military purposes in the bloody quarrels of the Great Powers.

For Great Britain herself the consequences would be scarcely less serious, if South West Africa once again fell into German hands. All text-books on imperial strategy written since the War emphasize the fact that the entire west coast of Africa is in the hands either of Britain or of friendly Powers, such as France, Portugal, and Belgium. To offer Germany two excellent harbours in Walvis Bay and Lüderitz would be to destroy that monopoly of control. Germany would be established in a flank position on the route to Australia and the East via the Cape which would become of great importance if, either from necessity or expediency, we were to abandon the Mediterranean route. Further, from bases in South West Africa German cruisers, submarines, or warplanes would be within easy striking distance of the great South American trade-route which converges on the African coast near the Cape Verde Islands. It is true that Germany would have some difficulty in maintaining bases in South West Africa since neither coal nor oil is produced locally. Nevertheless, to return South West Africa to the new

South West Africa

militarist Germany would gratuitously increase the already grave problems of imperial defence and trade protection. Even if Walvis Bay and Lüderitz could not be converted into first-class naval bases, one has only to remember the exploits of the *Emden* in the Indian Ocean to realize their possibilities as fuelling stations for raiding cruisers or submarines preying upon trade.

Strategic considerations are, therefore, of the utmost importance in considering the return of South West Africa to Germany, and the whole force of the strategic argument is emphatically directed against its return.

VI

TANGANYIKA

I

TANGANYIKA Territory, with an area of 260,000 square miles, is a vast but not a wealthy country. The total population amounts only to 9,000 whites and to some 5,000,000 natives, giving a density of population of 14·4 persons to the square mile. The coastal plain, extending approximately 500 miles from north to south, varies in width from 10 to 40 miles. Behind this tropical strip the country consists of a high plateau, which in the west falls steeply to the shores of Lakes Tanganyika and Nyasa. In the north-west, as well as in the south near Lake Tanganyika, the climate is comparatively favourable to European settlement.

Imperial Germany was a late arrival in East Africa, and it was not until 1885 that Karl Peters secured a charter to exploit the concessions that he had already obtained for the German East Africa Company from native chieftains in the Usagara country. Two years later his company had leased from the Sultan of Zanzibar the whole of the Tanganyika coast-line, which the Anglo-German agreement of 1886 had determined should fall within the German sphere of influence. The virtual independence of the coast Arabs, however, from the control of the Sultan, coupled with the fact that the Germans were complete

Tanganyika

new-comers and that the Hinterland behind their claim had the doubtful merit of being the flourishing source of the slave-trade, made Arab resistance much stiffer than it had been in British East Africa. Consequently, when the Company's officials attempted to take over the coast-line, their action provoked a serious revolt. Although suppressed, with British aid, this rising brought to light larger questions than could be dealt with by the Company's servants, and a German Protectorate was therefore proclaimed on 22 October 1889. Order was substantially established by 1890.

In this latter year, Count Caprivi, who had succeeded Bismarck as Imperial Chancellor, surrendered Germany's claims to Uganda, Witu, and Nyasaland to Great Britain in part return for Heligoland. None the less, he abandoned his predecessor's views on the colonial question, together with his aim 'to be the governing merchant rather than the governing bureaucrat. . . . Our privy councillors are excellent enough at home, but in the colonial territories I expect more from the Hanseatics who have been there'. Soon after the Heligoland Treaty the Imperial Government took over the full responsibility of administering the territory of the East African Company, and full sovereign rights over the coastal belt were purchased from the Sultan of Zanzibar.

The inexperience of the German officials and the presence in the Hinterland of strong, warlike races led almost at once to a number of native risings. The most serious of these were in the south, where the local Bantu tribes had learned the art of war from the Zulus. In 1891 the most powerful nation, the Wahehe, under Mkwawa, broke into a revolt which was not suppressed until 1894.

A number of years of peace followed, during which the authority of the Government was extended over the whole country. Discontent, however, was aroused by the introduction of a hut tax in 1897, and increased by the frequent demands for forced labour. Finally, in 1905, the so-called Maji-Maji rebellion broke out. The whole country between Lake Nyasa and the coast joined together in resisting the Germans, and was pacified only after two years of ruthless warfare, in which 70,000 natives perished in battle and a further 50,000 as a result of the destruction of their crops and villages by German troops.

Similar disturbances in the Cameroons (1904-5) and in South West Africa (1903-7) caused a separate colonial office to be created in Germany and saw the dawn of happier days in East Africa. Plans for more effective transport were at once put in hand. In the north, the existing Usambara railway was, by 1911, extended to Moshi, a distance of 220 miles from the coast, thus providing transport facilities for the European plantations that had sprung up in the Kilimanjaro highlands, and passing within 12 miles of the frontier of British East Africa. More important still was the line from Dar-es-Salaam, on the coast, inland. Morogoro (130 miles) was reached in 1907, and

Tanganyika

Kigoma, on the shores of Lake Tanganyika, 770 miles from the terminus at Dar-es-Salaam, in 1912.

Little administrative improvement accompanied this development in transport. In 1907 the Protectorate had been divided into three northern Residencies, where the inhabitants continued to be ruled by their Sultans under the supervision of German Residents, and into fourteen civil and two military departments. Here native administration was in the hands of paid native officials, and suffered from the defect that these officials possessed arbitrary powers while at the same time, being for the most part Arabs, they were out of sympathy with the native population. The German administrative staff was hopelessly inadequate; even in 1914 there were only 79 officials for an area of 395,000 square miles and a native population of 7,000,000. No system of indirect rule—except in the north—was contemplated, and the phrase 'an alien rule that frequently lacked the virtues of enlightenment' can truly be employed as a general description of German centralized control. Nor did the Germans grasp the limitations of flogging and of force as methods of government. Although such practices were greatly diminished after 1907, the flogging and chaining of criminals and those who had violated labour contracts continued until the end of German rule. On the other hand, some great technical progress was made. The Agricultural Institute, founded in 1912 at Amani in the Usambara mountains, the generous grants made to native education, hygiene, and agriculture, together with the settlement of 5,000 white immigrants in the north-east and the south-west will all bear witness to the activity of German rule.

During the War the German military commander, von Lettow Vorbeck, proved his ability as a soldier by keeping at bay the Allied forces, whose numbers ultimately reached 114,000, for the whole period of hostilities. Only after the Armistice did he surrender.

Throughout these years, however, the Germans showed little consideration for the native population, although the native troops upon which von Lettow Vorbeck relied must have been well looked after. The following is a description taken from Frank Cana's article in Vol. 17 of the *Journal of the African Society*:

'All the able-bodied men and youths they could lay hands upon, the Germans impressed either as soldiers or as carriers. The young women were given to their Askari; the children and old folk were left in their villages to starve. The carriers were used precisely as cattle; those incapable of further service were abandoned by the roadside to die. Border regions were depopulated; fearing that their inhabitants would aid the British, the Germans deported them without ceremony. Forced levies of food were made on tribes whom it was otherwise impossible to turn into service. . . .'

In 1919 the country was in a state of complete administrative chaos.

II

By the colonial settlement of 1919 Tanganyika was committed as a B Mandate to Great Britain; subse-

Tanganyika

quently a strip of territory, known as Ruanda-Urundi, in the north-west, was allocated under mandate to Belgium. Not only was the administration subjected to a certain amount of international control by the League of Nations, but since the territory lay within the conventional basin of the Congo, the obligations assumed by the British Government under the Berlin and Brussels Acts of 1885 and 1890 (renewed in the St. Germain-en-Laye Convention of 1919) also applied to the whole of Tanganyika.[1]

If the character of a B class Mandate is examined, it will be noticed that early self-determination is not envisaged. The administration, however, under the safeguards enumerated in Article 22, must be conducted with due regard to native laws and institutions. It will be worth while to examine a few of the provisions of the Mandate in detail.

Article 6 of the Tanganyika Mandate runs:

'The mandatory shall in the framing of laws relating to the holding or transference of land take into consideration native laws and customs, and shall respect the rights and safeguard the interests of the native population. No native land may be transferred, except between natives, without the previous consent of the public authorities, and no real rights over native land in favour of non-natives may be created except with the same consent. The mandatory will promulgate strict regulations against usury.'

The League favours indirect administration with a view to educating the natives towards self-govern-

[1] See the relevant articles of these Acts quoted in Appendix V.

ment. For this reason union with the adjacent territories is looked upon with suspicion, and Article 10 reads:

'The mandatory shall be authorised to constitute the territory into a customs, fiscal and administrative union or federation, with the adjacent territories under his own sovereignty or control, provided always that the measures adopted to that end do not infringe the provisions of this mandate.'

It should, however, be added that in 1926 the British Secretary of State for Colonies stated publicly that the tenure of the British was in the nature of a 'servitude' in the technical legal sense of that term, i.e. an obligation to observe certain rules with regard to administration, which differed only in degree from the obligation undertaken in Kenya and throughout the whole conception of trusteeship and administration of British dependencies.

There are a few other points which are of great concern in this Mandate. Thus in Article 3 it is laid down that the mandatory shall be responsible for the peace, order, and good government of the territory and shall undertake to promote to the utmost the material and moral well-being and the social progress of its inhabitants, with full powers of legislation and administration.

Article 7, dealing with equality in commerce, goes far to meet German economic arguments. It stipulates that there shall be complete equality in matters of residence, entry, property, trade, economic freedom, concessions, rights of companies, and associations.

Much criticism has been levelled at the Mandates system;[1] yet it should be remembered that the German claim is one for absolute ownership, which in no way envisages the continuation of the Mandate. The provisions outlined above, together with those embodied in the Congo Treaties, have done much to secure protection for the natives' interests. We have to face the prospect, if Tanganyika is restored to Germany, of seeing these limitations upon the administration swept away and the native population left to the mercies of a Government which has openly proclaimed its indifference to world opinion and which is entirely free from the challenge of criticism at home.

III

In spite of an energetic search during the past fifteen years, Tanganyika remains a comparatively unimportant source of minerals. In 1937 the value of all minerals sold locally and exported from Tanganyika amounted only to £652,442, of which gold accounted for no less than £526,338. It is apparent, therefore, that the mineral industry of Tanganyika is based on gold. There are at present five large gold-fields in Tanganyika. Some of them have promising future prospects. It is, in fact, expected that the Tanganyika gold output will exceed £1,000,000 per annum in a very short time. The future of this industry depends

[1] See *ante*, chap. II.

very largely, however, upon its ability to attract capital. Certain other minerals are produced in small quantities: salt (both on the coast and in the interior), diamonds, and tin. Such supplies of iron, coal, and lead as have been found are entirely negligible.

It is, however, almost certain that the future of Tanganyika lies not in its mining industry but in the development of agriculture. The climatic conditions vary so greatly that almost every crop could be raised in one part or other of the country. Agriculture, however, labours under considerable difficulties. It is troubled with pests like locusts and tsetse, and faces a serious problem in soil erosion. The Tanganyika government, supported by the Colonial Development Trust, has done much to overcome these disabilities, but much still remains to be done.

By far the most important commercial crop of Tanganyika is sisal, which was introduced by the Germans, but has been enormously extended under the British. In 1913 the value of sisal exports was £535,580. Last year the value was £2,079,204. There is every indication that sisal-growing will continue to increase. Next in importance among commercial crops comes cotton, the development of which has been, and is being, furthered by the Empire Cotton Growing Corporation. The value of cotton exports in 1913 was £120,753. In 1937 it was £603,594. Coffee comes third. The slopes of Kilimanjaro and other volcanic highland districts provide ideal conditions for the development of a large coffee trade, and it is almost certain that much further progress will be achieved in this field. The value of coffee exports in 1913 was £21,180. In 1937 it was £429,501. In addition, Tanganyika produces large quantities of ground-nuts, sesame, copra, and rice, in all of which the trend of production is upwards. In recent years, too, the production of tea has increased substantially. Among animal products, hides and skins play a substantial role in the country's trade, and amongst forestry products beeswax, gums, resins, and rubber add to its wealth.

We may conclude this section with the observation that, though very considerable economic development has taken place in Tanganyika during the past twenty years, much of the country's store of resources remains untouched. Owing to unfavourable natural conditions, intensive development will never prove an easy task, and must depend upon the country's ability to attract European capital.

Official figures for Germany's capital investments in Tanganyika for the immediate pre-War years are not available, but it appears that these investments considerably exceeded the actual trade surplus.[1] The period since 1922 has been one of immense progress for Tanganyika. The Central Railway from Dar-es-Salaam, the capital, to Kigoma on Lake Tanganyika, and the Tanga Railway from Tanga to Moshi, have

---

[1] According to Dr. Fränkel, *Capital Investment in Africa*, Oxford, 1938, there was £33,576,000 capital invested in German East Africa, most of which would be German (op. cit., Table 28).

been extended under British rule. The territory's railway system now extends for 2,077 kilometres, as against 1,435 kilometres in 1913. The country's roads, too, have been much improved and extended. The shipping services are more numerous and more efficient, and in addition the development of air navigation has proved helpful both in the development of internal communications and in the establishment of contacts between Tanganyika and the rest of the world, particularly the British Empire.

German East African exports reached their peak level in 1913, when products to the value of £1,773,000 were exported. Imports for 1913 were valued at £2,667,900. There was thus an unfavourable balance in the colony's trade of about £945,000. Germany largely dominated the country's trade in pre-War years. In 1912 Germany supplied slightly over 50 per cent. of the total imports, and took over 56 per cent. of the total exports.

The rise of Tanganyika's mineral industry, and particularly the development of its agriculture since the War, has enabled the country to raise its exports well above the level of imports. Since 1932 the country has always recorded favourable trade balances, exceeding £1,000,000 in each of the last two years. This achievement is remarkable in the light of to-day's imports, which now approach £4,000,000 a year, compared with less than £2,700,000 in the peak year of the German era. In 1937, for example, Tanganyika's total exports amounted to £5,311,464, a new high level and not much less than three times the record level of the pre-War period.

There are five products which dominate Tanganyika's export trade: the proportions of each of these in 1937 were as follows:

Sisal, 41·8 per cent.
Cotton, 12·1 per cent.
Gold, 10·6 per cent.
Coffee, 8·6 per cent.
Ground-nuts, 5·2 per cent.

Among Tanganyika's imports (which last year totalled £3,924,095), cotton piece goods are by far the most important class. They account for 20·5 per cent. of the total. Machinery follows with 6·7 per cent., and then come iron and steel manufacture and foodstuffs with 5·0 per cent. each, motor spirit with 4·7 per cent., building materials 4·5 per cent.

In pursuance of the terms of the Mandate Great Britain has maintained the 'Open Door' in Tanganyika since taking over control. The United Kingdom in 1937 only figured in Tanganyika's import trade to the extent of 24·3 per cent., and took only 29·9 per cent. of Tanganyika's exports. Japan supplied in 1937 no less than 23·8 per cent. of the country's total imports (mostly cotton piece goods), while taking only 0·2 per cent. of its exports. Germany is the third largest supplier of Tanganyika. She was responsible for 13·4 per cent. of the country's total imports, and for 10·1 per cent. of the exports. Between 1925 and

1937 Germany's total trade surplus with Tanganyika amounted to no less than £1,179,030.

IV

Although progress in public health administration during the past twenty years has been rapid, further extensions and improvement of health services are urgently needed in Tanganyika as elsewhere in equatorial Africa. The Government, unable to provide enough doctors and hospital accommodation for countless patients, is turning more and more to preventative measures against malaria, sleeping-sickness, hook-worm, and other tropical diseases. African dispensers and learners are trained to give simple medical and surgical aid, while the more advanced students are enabled by government grants to enter the medical school at Mulago in Uganda.

Success in the health services is bound up with education. Until recently there was a tendency to leave education in the hands of the various missionary societies. Much has been done by grants-in-aid to secure some uniformity of standard and some control of syllabus; nevertheless, it is becoming increasingly realized that it is unsatisfactory to leave anything but elementary education to the missions alone. Nor can the government ignore the large numbers of unbaptized children who at present receive no education whatsoever. Certain progress has, however, been made. While higher education has not been neglected, the authorities have aimed more and more at providing a practical education, which will produce a generation with more advanced ideas on hygiene, health, production of food, and of cash crops. There is to-day less insistence than formerly on purely literary education.

V

The history of settlement in East Africa by non-native peoples is long and intricate.[1] Already by the tenth century A.D. Arab invaders who had long traded down this coast had founded Kilwa, Mombasa, and Zanzibar. From then until the sixteenth century the Arabs controlled most of the East African coast, their power reaching the height of its prosperity between A.D. 1100 and 1300. Then in the sixteenth century came the Portuguese, who established their power over the east coast and ruled with the aid of tributary Arab sultans.

The Portuguese rule, however, was never very firmly founded, and in the late seventeenth century the Arabs of Oman and Muscat succeeded in driving them out, taking Mombasa in 1698. A shadowy allegiance to Muscat survived the eighteenth century, until in 1832 Seyyid Said transferred his capital from Muscat to Zanzibar. The Arab suzerainty became more of a reality and the Sultan's authority was spread over the whole of the coast area of Tanganyika and Kenya. At more or less the same time Indians were beginning to trade with Tanganyika and even to

[1] Reference should be made to Professor R. Coupland's recent book: *East Africa and its Invaders*, Oxford, 1938.

settle there. These facts explain the presence in Tanganyika of other races besides the Africans and the Europeans. In 1931 the Indians numbered 23,400, the Arabs 7,000, and the Goans 1,700, compared with no more than 8,000 Europeans.

The native tribes, the majority of them Bantu peoples, who, of course, form the largest part of the population, are divided between nine provinces. Their tribal organization is strong, a fact of great importance, since the success of 'indirect rule' very largely depends upon the strength and solidarity of the native community. The Lake Province is by far the most densely populated with 1,466,600 inhabitants. The Central and Mahenge provinces appear to be pestered by the tsetse-fly and in three years the population decreased by over 41,000. The natural economy of these tribes varies considerably. Eighteen of them are pastoral as well as agricultural peoples, sixteen practise agriculture only, and two are purely pastoral tribes.

The non-native peoples are mostly to be found in the coastal areas, especially the Eastern Province, where they derive a living from trade in such towns as Dar-es-Salaam and Tanga. Indeed, practically all the retail trade and a great deal of the import and export trade of the country is in Indian hands.

The policy of 'indirect rule', as followed in Tanganyika, means the attempt, while checking the worst abuses, to graft the rulers' civilization on the soundly rooted native stock; its aim is to foster what is best in

Tanganyika

native tradition and mould it into a form consistent with modern ideas, enlisting the real force of the spirit of the people in support of the administration. It can, of course, be successfully applied only where the aboriginal tribes were organized under strong chiefs; for otherwise it is necessary to draw together scattered units under a supreme chief, or to form native councils to which a large measure of self-government may be entrusted. Basically, indirect rule is sound, for all races of peoples prefer local self-rule to direct alien rule; but, if a system of government is to be permanent and progressive, it must be rooted in the indigenous framework.

The object must be to maintain intact native institutions and native autonomy—the chief and his council, districts and their headmen, who in turn control village heads. A Resident must act as sympathetic adviser and councillor to the chief, being careful not to lower his prestige, and not interfering with instructions to subordinate headmen.

'The native authority', says Lord Lugard,[1] 'is thus *de facto* and *de jure* ruler over his own people. He appoints and dismisses his subordinate chiefs and officials. He exercises the power of allocation of lands, and with the aid of native courts, of adjudication in land disputes and expropriation for offences against the community. The lawful orders which he may give are carefully defined by the ordinance, and in the last resort are enforced by the Government. Since native authority, especially if

[1] Lord Lugard, *The Dual Mandate in British Tropical Africa*, 1922, p. 203.

exercised by alien conquerors, is inevitably weakened by the first impact of civilised rule, it is made clear to the elements of disorder, who regard force as conferring the only right to demand obedience, that government, by the use of force if necessary, intends to support the native chief. To enable him to maintain order he employs a body of unarmed police, and if the occasion demands the display of superior force, he looks to the government. The native ruler derives his power from the Suzerain, and is responsible that it is not misused. He is equally with British officers amenable to the law, but his authority does not depend on the caprice of an executive officer. To intrigue against him is an offence punishable, if necessary, in a Provincial Court. Thus both British and Native Courts are invoked to uphold authority. The essential feature of the system is that the native chiefs are constituted as an integral part of the machinery of the administration. There are not two sets of rulers—British and Native—working either separately or in co-operation, but a single government in which the native chiefs have well-defined duties and an acknowledged status equally with British officials. Their duties should never conflict and should overlap as little as possible. They should be complementary to each other, and the chief himself must understand that he has no right to place any power unless he renders his proper services to the State.'

But there are limitations to this independence, rightly belonging to the controlling power as trustee for the welfare of the natives; they do not, however, imply interference with the chief's authority or the social structure. These limitations are the following:

1. The sole right to impose taxation in any form is

Tanganyika

reserved to the Suzerain power, although the native authority is responsible for the collection of the tax and retains from 20 to 33 per cent. of the proceeds for its own native treasury.

2. The right of legislation is reserved in the hands of the Central Government.

3. The right to appropriate land on equitable terms for public purposes and for commercial requirements is vested in the Governor.

4. All non-natives and natives not subject to the local native jurisdiction live in the 'township', from which natives subject to the native administration are as far as possible excluded. 'This exclusive control of aliens by the Central Government partakes rather of the nature of "extra-territorial jurisdiction" than of dualism,' states Lord Lugard.

The courts established are composed entirely of native judges. The law administered is the indigenous law, together with such English law as may be included in Rules drawn up by Court or Chief and approved by the Governor. There are a series of courts with various degrees of jurisdiction. Appeals lie from a lower to a higher court, and strictly speaking there is no appeal to the European provincial courts, although a district officer may make the transference or the Resident is empowered to revise judgements.

As a Group we feel very strongly that the experiment of indirect rule is of the greatest importance for the future of Africa. Here in Tanganyika an African community has been established which is well on its way to a civilization with its own peculiar characteristics and differing widely from that of any European country. The return of Tanganyika to an authoritarian government which openly declares its intention to pursue the rapid economic exploitation of its colonial territories would be fatal to the continuance of that community's existence. It is essential to preserve the system of indirect rule, and to ensure time for the fulfilment, or at least for the further trial, of a process which has been so successfully begun; and, apart from any other considerations, we feel that there could be no question of the transference of this territory to another régime, unless there were the most reassuring guarantees of the continuance of the present system. We see no evidence that any such guarantees would be given or even considered; and even if they were probable, we doubt whether they could be satisfactorily implemented by a changed national administration, even of the most sincere intentions.

The possibility of the transference of Tanganyika to Germany is far from being a remote academic possibility. Although much less is known and heard of the Nazi movement in Tanganyika than in South West Africa, such a movement undoubtedly exists and is increasing its influence in an alarming fashion. The basis for Nazi agitation is provided by the considerable German population in the Territory: out of a European population of 8,455 in 1935, 2,665 were Germans and a further 197 immigrated in that year. With the support of the Reich Colonial Department,

Tanganyika

new settlers are being sent out from Germany each year. Strict control over the German population is maintained by unofficial Nazi organizations and measures are taken against those who resist such regimentation. Particular care is taken to influence and impress the natives, many of whom appear to believe that the reappearance of Germany in East Africa is imminent. Especially within the last few months the Nazi sympathizers have become more vociferous. The movement is strongest in the north and in Iringa, but a feeling of apprehension is spreading throughout the country, which official pronouncements have done little to reassure. Insurance rates against the return of the territory to Germany are already being quoted and a substantial premium is being demanded. Clearly immediate and forceful action is called for on the part of the Administration, unless the Nazi agitation is to have the same harmful effects upon the general life of the community as it has had in South West Africa.

VI

The strategic importance of Tanganyika in any scheme of imperial defence has already been pointed out in Part I. The defensive strength of her military position was demonstrated in the last war; to-day the restoration of Tanganyika to German control, with the probable dissemination of anti-British propaganda, could hardly fail to prove the offensive possibilities of the territory and to weaken our own position in East Africa.

Commercially, Tanganyika controls Lakes Victoria, Nyasa, and Tanganyika, to which the lateral railway from the west affords ready access. The territory is, therefore, a valuable highway to the interior of Africa. Tanganyika also lies across the present Empire air-route from Great Britain to the Cape, which goes via Khartoum and Nairobi. Northern Tanganyika is entered at Moshi, and the route passes from north to south across the territory, through Dodoma and so to Nyasaland. Off the Tanganyika coast, at Zanzibar, cable communication is maintained with Great Britain, and the Seychelles Island, farther out to sea, is an important cable junction between Great Britain, South Africa, and the East. German rule in Tanganyika would directly menace our air service, at once put an end to all Cape to Cairo railway projects, and, in the event of hostilities, perhaps threaten imperial cable communications. It would also make the Rhodesias, and, more particularly, the wealth of the Rand, vulnerable to long-distance bombing.

Tanganyika's strategical importance has been enhanced by the recent expansion of the Italian Empire in East Africa. The significance of the Rome-Berlin axis cannot be ignored; were Tanganyika handed back to Germany, Kenya, Uganda, and the Sudan would be hemmed in by German or Italian possessions and British control of the Suez–Red Sea route to the Far East would be weakened. The presence of a German-Italian wedge in East Africa would mean that we might, in time of war, lose the 'back-door' route to Egypt and the Sudan—the land route north from South Africa.

Further, our maritime communications with South Africa and the East, both via the Suez Canal and the Cape itself, would be threatened by the establishment of a potentially hostile control in Tanganyika. The remarkable successes of the *Emden* spell a warning against the future presence of German warships or submarines in the Indian Ocean, especially if they had a harbour or head-quarters such as Tanganyika could provide.

The hostile attitude of Japan towards Britain, not to speak of her growing friendship with Germany, has threatened our naval position generally, and in the Pacific particularly. Under existing conditions we are able to maintain very small naval squadrons on the Cape, the East Indies, and the Australian stations, and still to enjoy a clear supremacy in the Indian Ocean. If, as we have indicated above, German naval forces were stationed on the east coast of Africa, our strategic position in the Indian Ocean would be vastly complicated, with far-reaching consequences for our far-eastern schemes of defence.

The question of ocean and air communications is thus of serious import when considering the possible rendition of Tanganyika in terms of British Commonwealth security. But it may well be that in this regard the decisive factor is the attitude of the Union of South Africa. For her, the paramount objective in the Great War was the conquest of the German colonies in order to effect the removal of an alien Power, which threatened to curb and possibly dominate her national expansion. From the position that the Union was the representative of white civilization in the southern half of the African Continent the transition was almost inevitable to the standpoint that she must be its *sole* champion and propagator in that area. 'We shall leave to our children', declared General Smuts in 1915, 'a huge country, in which to develop a type for themselves, and to form a people who will be a true civilizing agency in this dark continent.'[1] In a parallel situation the Republic of the United States, also young and no less virile, did not rest until it had got rid of the authority of a foreign Power at its southern gateway of Louisiana, and in due time proclaimed an embargo upon any European interference in any part of the American continents.

This sense of 'High destiny' is reinforced in the case of South Africa by the conviction that its success, and her own ultimate existence, depend upon the stamping of the imprint of her distinctive culture upon the primitive peoples who constitute the vast majority of her population. The imprint is copyright: and no other—however similar—must be used.

In consequence, the Union agreed to abandon annexation for a C Mandate over South West Africa only with extreme reluctance. And when the German population of that region steadily refused to be assimilated, and indeed proclaimed a dual allegiance, the

[1] S. G. Millin, *General Smuts*, vol. i, p. 237.

sense of insecurity and of menace to the national destiny thus engendered gave rise to a deepening determination to prevent the re-entry of the unwelcome rival into the northern as well as the western gateway.

This view was strongly expressed by the South African members of the Group, and there is abundant evidence from the public utterances of their statesmen that it is representative. It does not arise from antipathy to Germany or to Germans, with whom Afrikanders claim some degree of racial affinity. Indeed, a certain sympathy might be expected between a totalitarian régime and the Union Government, which share the view that an aristocratic exclusiveness of race is the only sound basis on which to civilize backward peoples. It is this circumstance which explains why South African politicians declare their unalterable determination to keep Germany out of Tanganyika, while at the same time supporting the claim that Germany has a right to a place in the sun —but in some other quarter of the African horizon.

Under certain conditions the United Kingdom might be induced to risk the weakening of her strategic position by surrendering Tanganyika, but before doing so she would be obliged to weigh a further possibility in the departure of the Union from the Commonwealth.

VII

THE CAMEROONS

I

THE British Mandate section of the Kamerun is a narrow strip of country south-east of the River Benue, reaching inland from the Gulf of Guinea for several hundred miles. On the south it is bordered by that section of the Kamerun which is now under French Mandate. Physically, the country consists of a low coastal plain, swampy and malarial, rising first to a belt of jungle, then to open grasslands towards Lake Chad. In the south-east are heavily wooded lowlands. It is well watered, the rainfall on the slopes of Mount Cameroon itself being the heaviest in Africa. The chief resources therefore are those from trees—rubber, palm nuts and kernels, and certain timbers. Cacao is grown in higher parts, and on the inland plains there is good pasturage. There are a few minerals but these are of little value. At one time, before the elephants were killed off, quite valuable stores of ivory were obtained.

Up to 1911 the area of German Kamerun was 190,000 square miles; in that year, by a treaty with France, it was increased to 292,000 square miles with a population of 2,650,000.[1] This consisted, in the

---

[1] These figures are given by H. R. Rudin, *Germans in the Cameroons*, London, 1938. Dr. Townsend, op. cit., gives different figures. See further, Appendix IV.

southern part, of Bantu-speaking and Negro (Sudanic-speaking) peoples, divided into many small tribes of different cultures and dialects. Here the Duala Bantu were the most important tribe. In the northern plains, first conquered by Haussa and later by the Fulbe, were kingdoms organized on a feudal plan. These were Islamic, and at the time of the German occupation Islam was moving south.

From the time of Herodotus 'Europeans' had been trading with the natives of the Guinea Coast. Later it was a reservoir for the slave-trade to America. In the nineteenth century it was an important centre of trade for various nations; and in the second half of the century English, French, Spanish, and Belgians began to assume sovereignty over various areas and in them to discriminate in favour of their own nationals. The area which later became Kamerun was traded in chiefly by English and Germans, with French encroaching from the south. There was a consular court headed by an English official, which settled disputes between whites and blacks. By 1880 the English consul's authority was considered necessary in order to establish a native chief properly in his position.

In the early eighties native chiefs had repeatedly begged to be taken under English protection. By 1884 the English Government, moved by fear of French influence, was slowly extending its protection, when suddenly the German Government presented it with a *fait accompli* in the form of treaties by which the coastal chiefs accepted German rule. Bismarck was reluctant to adopt a colonial programme; he did so, under pressure from commercial interests, in order to keep an area free for German trade. Feeling between England and Germany ran high, but differences were adjusted. Since traders, especially Woermann, had induced the German Government to assume sovereignty in the Kamerun, their influence remained powerful throughout the period of German rule.

II

Rule was gradually extended to the interior. The Government at first tried to persuade traders to extend German influence; but in the end advance had to be made by force, especially as the Duala Bantu possessed, under their treaty with Germany, vested commercial interests of which the traders wished to deprive them. These Duala had abandoned their peasant life to act as middlemen between the traders on the coast and the natives of the interior. One of the conditions on which they accepted German protection was that this trade should not be interfered with. As the white traders moved inland they induced the Government to break this undertaking, though to the end, despite pressure from the traders, the Government protected the Haussa middlemen in the interior. In the Bantu areas, as they were conquered, military rule was replaced by civil rule in which the native authorities were allowed to play some part. But in the

The Cameroons

northern feudal kingdoms, which were well organized, the Government found it more economical to rule through the native organization by means of advisers appointed to the chiefs. In general, the administration interfered directly as little as possible with native customs, though missionaries were encouraged, save among the Mohammedans. But the heavy recruitment of labour, especially for porterage and for work on the plantations, shattered the native social organization.

The Governor was the head of the local administration. He was responsible to the Chancellor who, in colonial affairs, was largely independent of the Reichstag, though Socialist and Centre deputies were highly critical of colonial rule throughout. They, to a certain extent, secured the amelioration of policy. The Colonial Society, representing the growing German interest in colonies, had some voice, but, to the end, it was the traders who had the greatest influence. They were opposed by the planters, who competed with them for labourers, and both these exploiting groups were opposed by the missionaries. At first a syndicate of traders advised the Government, but it was disintegrated by the conflicting interests of rival firms. The role of the Government came to be that of umpire between these quarrelling exploiters, and to a certain extent, in order that it might protect itself against criticism from either side, its policy was determined by the interests of the natives. This became particularly noticeable after 1907, when a Colonial Office was created under Dernburg, though the change of policy was also influenced by liberal criticisms in the Reichstag.

The traders were in Kamerun frankly to make what they could out of the land and the natives, and their power was sufficient to control the acts of the Government. They prevented the Government putting a stop to the trade in guns and liquor for a long time, and two big firms flagrantly disobeyed Government attempts to control the granting of credit facilities to natives. They obstructed a law to prohibit the employment of women as carriers. They even entered areas which had been quarantined by medical officers because of small-pox, since they hoped that their rivals would stay away and leave them a clear field for big profits. Their servants would leave trade goods in a native's hut and tell him that he must soon have a commensurate supply of rubber or he would be punished. Their attitude, as the administration complained, was wholly inconsistent. They insisted on selling guns to the natives and at the same time demanded protection from native attacks. The traders' ingenious defence of this arms trade was that they sold only old flintlocks, not modern rifles, and that the natives, confidently attacking with their obsolete weapons, in the open, were more easily shot than when they fought from the bush with native weapons.

Between 1890 and 1900 plantations in the Kamerun increased apace. The planters grew the same things as the traders bought, but their quarrels were over the limited supply of labour and not over the market for their goods. By 1914 100,000 hectares of the best land on the highlands were under cultivation. At first the death-rate of labourers on these plantations was very high, but it was gradually reduced as the Government began to control the conditions of employment, despite the planters' protests; though an administrative attempt to ensure that labourers would not be taken to work in places climatically different from their homes, to the injury of their health, was frustrated. Of these plantations it may be noted that the Hailey African Survey states that in West Africa 'cacao is native grown, except in the Cameroons, where large plantations, some of which continue to be exploited by European owners, were established under the German rule. . . . German policy attached value to a system of large policy plantations as a means to the rapid development of coffee plantations and rubber plantations in the Cameroons'.[1] And Dr. Fränkel concludes that 'where mineral, or relatively easily exploited sylvan resources, are lacking it has become increasingly clear that development depends on the creation of systems of peasant production, and the introduction of new products, and new economic methods'.[2] Any other method of production results in the ruthless exploitation of the native population and ultimately its demoralization and depletion. This explains the nature of the charges brought by an early German writer against a certain Governor, because

[1] *An African Survey*, Oxford, 1938, at pp. 907 and 981.
[2] S. H. Fränkel, *Capital Investment in Africa*, Oxford, 1938, p. 13.

he had given his officials too much freedom in the last few years and, instead of laying the main stress on developing native industry, had favoured plantations. The experience of the neighbouring English colonies, where the cocoa-planting interests were in the hands of the natives and had developed far more than in the Kameruns, seemed to show this to be the better method.[1] It is significant that both the large chartered companies established in Kamerun, despite their wide powers over land and men, failed.

The chief difficulty in exploiting the wealth of the Kameruns was the lack of communications, and the building of two railways did not altogether solve this problem. At one time 85,000 men, women, and children were carrying goods on one road. Not only was their own village life shattered, but their uncontrolled depredations on the villages along the road for food or women disturbed native life throughout the country. They were a potent factor in the spread of venereal and other diseases. A pro-German writer concludes that the natives 'were well treated' under German rule. But his statement that 'a student cannot escape the conviction that everything was being done by Germany to get the maximum from the Colony' contrasts curiously with his claim if one remembers, in his own words, that 'native policy was determined by the view that in the task of exploiting... resources, the greatest asset was the native'. Clearly, the writer

[1] A. Zimmerman, *Geschichte der Deutschen Kolonialpolitik*, Berlin, Ernst Siegfried Mittler und Sohn, 1914.

The Cameroons

has in mind not the natives' own interests, nor even the ultimate interests of the colony, but the immediate interest of the exploiters.[1] This policy was vigorously enforced by governors like Puttkamer; Seitz, on the other hand, genuinely strove for the natives' welfare, though he was continually frustrated by his Advisory Council of traders and planters. The lot of the natives seems to have varied according to the character of the Governor. It is fair to say that the Government attempted, save under certain Governors, to ameliorate the conditions of the natives—for example, it passed laws to control the flogging of the natives, and the number of convictions for this offence show not only the vigour of its policy in this respect, but the urgent need for that policy. But the chief restraints on the exploiters were the missionaries and the liberal deputies in the Reichstag. The pro-German writer cited above states that the missionaries were the chief agents of education; they were on the whole opposed by the traders and planters, and by Governors such as Puttkamer, who would not listen to them. 'It may rightly be said that missionaries were often the natives' only protection against inconsiderate administrators and exploiters.'[2] As noted above, the opinion of liberal deputies in the Reichstag was also of some weight.

Apart from direct administrative work the Government supported schools and health services for the

[1] H. R. Rudin, *Germans in the Cameroons, 1884–1914*, London, Cape, 1938, at pp. 277, 297, a good account of the history, but lacking in all judgement and remarkable for its misunderstanding of native life.

[2] Rudin, op. cit., pp. 377–8.

natives and Germans; it also inaugurated admirable experimental work in tropical botany. Against this must be set the spirit in which the military subjection of the country was undertaken. Even Rudin states that German officers boasted unnecessarily of their triumphs over unarmed natives,[1] and this accords with Zimmermann's conclusion that, apart from the loss in human life and the high costs of military expeditions into the interior, growing disapproval in Germany was aroused because it gradually became known that the frequently careless and reckless behaviour of whites was mainly responsible for native uprisings. The writings of the murdered Loymeyer, for example, revealed that very energetic measures against the persons guilty of such actions were made one of the Government's duties. It appeared that often the ardent desire of young officers and officials to win military distinction was not without influence on the military measures.[2]

The labour position was far from being satisfactory. Owing to the shortage of labour, treaties with the defeated tribes always included provisions for the supply of forced labour to the Government. Moreover, a poll-tax was imposed on all males above the age of puberty, and to meet the demands of this tax, the native, who saw his land increasingly encroached upon, was practically compelled to work. Taxation and the shortage of land combined to produce a strong incentive to seek work.

[1] Rudin, op. cit., p. 310. [2] Zimmermann, op. cit., p. 259.

III

Despite the criticism which has been levelled against the German administration in Kamerun—for which indeed his book offers considerable confirmatory evidence—Mr. Rudin still appears to believe that the treatment of the natives was not altogether ungenerous. He points out, for instance, that during Puttkamer's governorship the natives were moved on to reservations, and he states that during that process they were treated as kindly as possible and were allowed to delay moving until they had reaped their crops in their old lands or until crops had ripened in their new lands. More than this, it was said that natives who moved into reservations other than those allotted to them were not punished, and, in some cases, were even given land in excess of what the law required. Yet in 1906 this same Governor, Puttkamer, was summoned before the Imperial Diet to answer grave charges of maladministration, of which he was found guilty, and the Puttkamer affair was one of the most serious of the 'colonial scandals' which led to the reorganization of the colonial administration in 1906–7 under Dr. Dernburg. At times, indeed, it is difficult to avoid the impression that Mr. Rudin's conclusions are in conflict with the evidence he himself adduces.

It has been said that the natives accepted the German rule at least with resignation. But their resignation seems to have been due more to the conviction that complaints were unavailing than to the belief that there was nothing about which to complain. To the missionaries, in fact, the natives repeated many grievances. The treatment which those who made official complaints received at the hands of the Administration was such as to discourage repetition of the experiment. Certain incidents in Kamerun history may be taken to illustrate the truth of this judgement.

In the nineties, under Acting-Governor Leist, there was a rising of police, due, as it later appeared, to his abusive treatment of them and their wives. Leist was tried in Germany and found guilty. The sentence, however, was commuted, and he was appointed to a position equal in rank, but lower in pay, although public opinion made it impossible for him to remain in Germany.[1] Again, in September 1905, a number of chiefs sent petitions simultaneously to the Reichstag and the Chancellor. They contained twenty-four complaints against the Administration. The Colonial Department sent this document to be dealt with, and reported on, by the officials of the régime which was the cause of complaint. The result was that, on their side, the accused officials demanded that the Governor punish their accusers. The latter were arrested and an investigation was opened against them. A judge, himself one of those against whom complaint had been made, was in charge of the investigation. On 6 December 1905 all the native petitioners were sentenced to long periods of imprisonment with hard labour.

[1] Cf. Rudin, op. cit., pp. 210–12.

This sentence was put before the Colonial Department because the Governor did not dare, after all the notice which the petition had received, to confirm it himself. The officials of the Colonial Department, so far as is known, supported the Kamerun judge. They vindicated the arrest and imprisonment of the chiefs, because otherwise they would have fled and caused disturbances. These officials further held that the complaints were partly without basis because the measures complained of were essential for good health. 'Besides this, one did not want the negroes to get the idea that they could put anything through in Berlin against the Government.' Later the case was reopened, and provoked so violent a discussion in the Reichstag that Governor Puttkamer was recalled.[1]

Two other cases are interesting reflections of this attitude. In 1907 the Akwa people sent a representative to Germany to plead their cause against taxation; even the liberal Governor Seitz threatened their leaders with exile if they persisted in their opposition, and in the end they were punished for making a levy to pay the expenses of their representative.[2] This was held to be usurping the functions of the Government. The trouble with these people reached its climax just before the War. They were to be moved from their homes because it was stated that their mode of life threatened the European settlement at Duala, though Rudin notes that the Government was possibly also influenced by the value of the land. A Government

[1] Zimmermann, op. cit., p. 260.   [2] Rudin, op. cit., p. 340.

doctor who protested against the measure was dismissed. The missionaries protested. Finally the chiefs telegraphed the Reichstag, but the Administration delayed the telegram while the measures were being carried out. The Reichstag objected to this procedure and orders were given that no such delay should occur again. The chief of the Duala Bantu tried to organize other tribes against the Government, and is said to have contemplated appealing to the British for protection. He was arrested and executed just before the War.[1]

At its best the German administration, however good its intentions, was hampered and frustrated by the opposition of the traders; at its worst, it simply allowed a free hand to the economic exploitation of the natives. Yet, in fact, from an economic point of view, the possession of Kamerun was more of a liability than an asset to Germany. In the last year of the German rule, when the revenue totalled 15,340,000 marks, the deficit to be made up on the colony's expenditure amounted to 6,940,000 marks, and imports (34,241,000 marks) considerably exceeded exports (23,336,000 marks). Possibly the continuation of German rule might have seen improvements: some progress had already been made since 1906, and in 1913 Dr. Solf, Minister for Colonies, was proposing to introduce some form of indirect rule in the colony. But the traders were strongly entrenched, and their opposition must unquestionably have retarded, even if

[1] Rudin, op. cit., pp. 408–13.

The Cameroons

it did not altogether frustrate, the Government's plans. In fact, however, the War broke out and Kamerun was occupied before the lines of future development became clear. The invasion of the territory by British and French troops met with considerable resistance, but by March 1916 the conquest had been completed and a temporary administration had been established which lasted until the Peace Settlement.

IV

After the War the former German colony of Kamerun became a mandated territory under a B Mandate and was divided into the French and British Cameroons. By the Milner-Simon Agreement of July 1919 the British were made responsible for the part adjoining the eastern frontier of Nigeria—with an area of some 34,080 square miles—and the French for the rest of the country, some 143,514 square miles in extent. Our concern here is only with the British Cameroons, a country only about one-fifth of the size of the German colony of Kamerun.

The fact that Nigeria adjoins the Cameroons has had a very considerable influence upon the political development of the mandated territory since the War. The three northern provinces—Kentu, Adamawa, and Dikwa—are administered with the Northern Provinces of Nigeria; and throughout the whole territory the Nigerian system of native administration known as 'indirect rule' is in force. The four southern districts of Victoria, Kumba, Mamfe, and Bamenda form a self-contained administrative unit—the Cameroons Province—under its own resident. It is in this, the coastal region, that political and economic development has made the greatest advance.

The method of 'indirect rule', by its very nature, cannot be a rigid and stereotyped administrative system. It will vary considerably from district to district. 'The one essential condition is that the native authority, whatever its form, must be able to command and receive the obedience of the people under its control.'[1] Even in a comparatively small country like the Cameroons wide variations of type are found. Frequent 'Intelligence' investigations are made with the object of collecting more accurate information about the historical customs and institutions of the tribes or clans; from the data thus provided schemes are devised for the better administration of the district in close accord with native institutions and life. Some idea of the varying forms of government is given by Lord Hailey:[2]

'In the coast area of Victoria District, the district head is an educated man, and head of one clan, whose authority extends over a heterogeneous population and does not rest upon native tradition; the Bakweri and Balong native authorities, also in the Victoria Division, are, on the other hand, based upon indigenous institutions, and consist of village heads with councils of elders, which send representatives to a clan council under the chair-

[1] Official Report of the Administration of the Cameroons under British Mandate, 1936.
[2] Hailey, *An African Survey*, pp. 433-4.

The Cameroons

manship of the district head. In parts of the Kumba Division the recognised native authorities are the representatives of small kindred groups which do not acknowledge a superior authority; in the Bamenda and Mamfe Divisions there are sometimes chiefs with councils, and in other areas the authority is the native court, consisting of representatives of the villages. In part of the Adamawa District, which the Lamido, the Fulani ruler, formerly controlled through hereditary fief-holders, it has been necessary to retain the system of district heads, though they are not hereditary leaders, since the pagan tribes are not yet able to provide leaders of their own. In the Kentu areas which are still in process of organization, chiefs and elders function as native authorities and courts. In Dikwa the standing of the Shehu closely resembles that of the emirs of Northern Nigeria; the Dikwa and Bornu ruling houses have indeed a common history. The Shehu is the native authority and controls the areas under his jurisdiction through district heads whom he appoints. He maintains his own police and his own prison.'

This last case, of the Shehu of Dikwa, is interesting as showing the influence of Islam. In fact about a quarter of the native population are Mohammedans.

Political organization is, in general, much more advanced and intricate in the southern area, the Cameroons Province, where some 407,690 natives, roughly a half of the total population, live and where European influence has been most active. The two principal powers enjoyed by the native authority, apart from ordinary administrative work, are financial and judicial. Between 50 per cent. and 60 per cent. of the general tax is allocated to the native treasuries, and at the end of 1937, despite considerable expenditure, all the native treasuries had surplus balances. What this means to the native in allowing him a substantial measure of self-government may be illustrated by the case of the Balong native authority in the Victoria Division. The authority here rests in the hands of the District Head, Fritz Mukete, assisted by a council. Under their control are four villages, each with a village court, and the right of appeal to the clan court at Muyuka. The clan started with £668 granted to them by the Victoria Native Administration, this sum representing the area's savings for past years. In 1936–7 the revenue was £690 and the expenditure £562. Out of this sum they maintained a school, a dispensary, a forest guard, their administrative buildings, and the salaries of their judicial and administrative staff.

The Official Report for 1936 remarked that in the eyes of the native the native courts still remained the most impressive and the most important side of 'indirect rule'. By the Native Courts Ordinance, 1933, the Nigerian judicial system was extended to the Cameroons. By this the native courts are graded into four different classes:

- A: with full powers for all civil and criminal cases, although no death penalty may be carried out until the Governor has confirmed the sentence.
- B: with full powers for civil cases involving amounts up to £100 and for criminal cases

with an adequate penalty of 1 year's imprisonment or £50 fine.

C: for civil cases involving amounts up to £50 and for criminal cases with penalties of 6 months' imprisonment or £10 fine.

D: for civil cases involving amounts up to £25 and for criminal cases with penalties of 3 months' imprisonment or £5 fine.

In 1937 there were in the British Cameroons 80 native courts of Grade D, 3 of Grade C, and 2 of Grade B. The Resident and District Officers have at all times the right of entry into native courts, and they can intervene to review the sentence, to order a retrial, or to transfer the case to a higher court. No sentence, however, can be increased, nor any order made to the prejudice of a party concerned, unless that party has first been given an opportunity to state his case. No native court possesses jurisdiction in cases of treason, sedition, official corruption, or revenue offences.

Despite these limitations—which are both equitable and necessary—the system of native courts works remarkably well. In 1936 they dealt with 9,697 civil cases, of which only 463 were reviewed and 236 modified after the review, a percentage of 2·4. In the same year, out of 3,347 criminal cases only 324 came up for review, and in only 166 cases was the sentence changed, a percentage of 4·9. These figures bear eloquent testimony to the success of the scheme. In all cases there is a right of appeal to a Magistrates' Court, and beyond that to the High Court and the

West African Court of Appeal. In less advanced areas the appeal lies to the District Officer, the Resident, or the Governor.

Like the judicial system, taxation in the British Cameroons follows very closely Nigerian practice. Between the northern areas of Kentu, Dikwa, and Adamawa, and the southern Cameroons Province there are, however, certain differences in assessment and collection. In the north each village or tribal unit is assessed at a certain lump sum, the distribution of individual contributions being left to the native authority: in the south this method has been gradually replaced by that of a flat rate. Collection in both cases is made by the native chiefs or councils, but the flat rate appears to be the more popular form of assessment with the natives. In Dikwa and Adamawa about one-third of the total tax comes from the *jangali* or tax on cattle, at a standard rate of 1s. 6d. per head of cattle. The general tax in the three northern provinces averages 3s. 3d., 3s. 4d., and 4s. 6d. per adult male: in the Cameroons Province the figures are generally higher, ranging from 1s. in the Bamenda Division to 8s. in Victoria. About 50 per cent. of the revenue from these taxes goes to the native treasuries, and the collection appears to be made without much difficulty.[1]

V

The economic development of the Cameroons has, in accordance with the policy of trusteeship, tended

[1] Figures from Lord Hailey, *An African Survey*, pp. 583–4.

The Cameroons

to be subordinated to the interests of the native peoples. The German plantations were, after the War, put up for auction and were largely repurchased by their former owners. According to the Annual Report of 1936 there are now 293,678 acres in German and 19,053 in British hands. There is no Government recruiting for private enterprise and the question of forced labour does not arise, the voluntary labour supply being more than sufficient. In 1937 there were 19,590 native wage-earners. Under the Nigerian Labour Regulations no native is allowed to work more than ten hours a day. Supervision of the labourers' conditions is conducted by the Government, and there is a system of medical inspection. The more serious problems of native labour are absent in the Cameroons, largely, perhaps, because there is now no mining in the territory.

Apart from the European-owned plantations, interesting experiments in native cocoa production have been initiated in the Kumba and Mamfe districts. In Kumba 93 cocoa-producing 'societies' are affiliated to a co-operative union, which had 1,568 members and sold 456 tons of cocoa in 1936. This society finances the cultivation as well as the sale of cocoa, and over £3,000 was loaned to finance production in 1936. In this, as in so many other matters, practice in the Cameroons is based upon the success of similar experiments in Nigeria and other parts of West Africa.

In general the policy of the British Government in

West Africa has been to limit land-alienation severely and to develop the country by peasant-cultivation. In the Cameroons the Germans, by the Decree of 15 June 1896, insisted that all land to which no claim could be legally maintained should be considered as Crown land. This regulation laid the onus of proof upon the native and was detrimental to his interests. The case of the North-west Cameroon Concession is quoted by Lord Hailey[1] as an illustration of the evils of this system: its result was that rights were conferred over all land which might at any time become Crown land—a contingent grant, the validity of which the British Government refused to recognize. Under the present policy the whole territory is regarded as native land. By the British Cameroons Administration Ordinance 1 of 1925, which extends the land law of Northern Nigeria to the mandated territory, alienation of land to non-natives can only be in the form of leases, not of freehold, and no such alienation can be made without the consent of the Governor. The actual amount of land in the hands of non-natives in 1936 was 539·4 square miles.

The economy of the country is completely agricultural, there being an export trade in five different products—bananas, rubber, cocoa, palm-oil and palm nuts, wood and timber. The prosperity of the territory is shown in the export figures for 1937, which record an increase of 18 per cent. over 1936: in the same period imports rose by 35 per cent. The pro-

[1] *African Survey*, p. 774.

duction of both bananas and rubber is expanding. In 1937 there was a 10 per cent. rise in the exports of bananas from the port of Tiko, bringing the figure up to 55,184 tons. The exports of rubber in 1937 amounted to 1,623,407 lb. (£36,353) as compared with 1,303,323 lb. (£20,585) in 1936. Cocoa and palm-oil exports were affected by serious falls in prices: cocoa, which in January 1937 fetched £39 a ton, in December could only fetch £15. 15s. On the whole, however, the country shows unmistakable signs of increasing prosperity. A useful index figure is the amount of the trade passing through the two ports of Victoria and Tiko: the total trade (export and import) of both ports in 1931 amounted to £259,298, in 1937 it reached £856,199—in six years over three times as much as in 1931.

The imports into the country are much the same as for any tropical country—to mention the more important: machinery, clothing, petrol and kerosene, rice, salt, tobacco, sacks, cement. One fact about the trade of the British Cameroons must, however, be emphasized—the importance of Germany both in the export and import trade of the country. Three countries figure largely in the import trade—the United Kingdom, which supplies 11·9 per cent. of the imports, Germany with 47·57 per cent., and Japan with 16·01 per cent.[1] In the export trade Germany practically dominates the market with 79·75 per cent., as compared with only 6·4 per cent. taken

[1] Figures from the Official Report, 1937.

by the United Kingdom. It was pointed out above that most of the plantations are still in German hands: indeed, out of the total European population of 408, 253 are Germans and only 75 English. These facts account in part for the importance of Germany in the country's trade. What we would point out, however, is that the German complaint of exclusion from colonial markets is certainly not applicable to the British Cameroons. The obligations of the mandate to maintain the 'Open Door' have been strictly kept, and the Germans, it is clear, have made the fullest use of their opportunities.

VI

In the Cameroons, as in most African colonies, much good work for education has been done by the Missionary Societies. Before the War, as we have seen, they were the strongest educational influence in the Cameroons. Their work, however, was practically confined to the coastal areas: in the north there were Moslem 'Koran schools', but in the centre, in Adamawa, nothing at all was done for education. Since the War the Missionary Societies have continued and augmented their work for education. In 1925 the British Government defined its attitude towards the missionary schools: it proposed neither to absorb these schools into its own system nor to leave them independent. They are required to conform to Government standards in education, but, if this is satisfactorily performed, they are to maintain their independent character, the Government supplementing their work by establishing its own schools.

One of the most important factors in the efficacy of a native educational policy must be the success of the Administration in winning the support and co-operation of the natives themselves. To a considerable extent this has been achieved in the Cameroons, where the native administrations maintain their own schools and where the demand for increased educational facilities is growing rapidly. The problems of native education are many and varied: they have been recently restated by Lord Hailey[1] and we do not propose to deal with them in detail. The principle was laid down in 1925 by the Advisory Committee on Native Education, that, 'Education should be adapted to the mentality, aptitudes, occupations and traditions of the various peoples, conserving as far as possible all sound and healthy elements in the fabric of their social life.' What means are the best to implement such a policy is a matter of controversy: the merits of vocational or literary training, the African's desire to receive a European education, the extension of girls' schools, especially in a country like the Cameroons with a large Moslem population, these are only a few of the problems which have to be faced in all the African colonies.

In the Cameroons Province attention has been concentrated upon providing elementary education. There are three different types of schools, those main-

[1] *African Survey*, chap. xviii.

tained by the Government, by the Native Authority, or by the Mission Society. The majority of the schools are Mission schools, 210 in all, of which 15 are state-assisted. The Government itself maintains 5 large elementary schools, and the various Native Authorities 19. In addition, there is a teachers' Training Centre at Kabe. The numbers of the children enrolled in 1937 were 8,007[1] in the Mission schools, 1,507 in the Native Administration schools, and 1,028 in the Government schools. The type of training given in these schools varies considerably; some of the Mission schools offer only the most simple teaching in the vernacular, while on the other hand there are mixed schools, like the Government school at Buea, where much of the instruction is given in English and where a remarkably high standard is attained. One interesting feature of the system is the provision of education for girls. When this was first proposed it met with considerable opposition, but there are now over 1,200 girls attending schools in the Cameroons Province.

Government expenditure in 1937 on education amounted to £14,298; the expenditure of the Native Authorities in the same year was £2,440. Much, however, remains to be done, and two criticisms can be made of the present system—one is the almost complete neglect of the Northern Districts, the other is the failure to provide any institution in the Cameroons where higher education can be given. At pre-

[1] This figure is for 1936, the others for 1937.

sent, those who desire a more advanced training must go to one of the two principal Nigerian colleges at Yaba, near Lagos, or at Kaduna, in Northern Nigeria. This criticism is not, however, so serious as the other: the neglect of the Northern Provinces is indeed striking. According to the Official Report for 1937 there is no school at all in Kentu, where pupils must attend classes outside the district. The state of affairs is very little better in Adamawa, though there are now four elementary schools in the Dikwa Division. This disparity of treatment between the north and the south, which runs through the whole of the Cameroons administration, should be remedied and adjusted at once.

In the field of public health, no less than in that of education, one of the most important, yet difficult, tasks is to gain the confidence and co-operation of the native. With increasing success—especially in the south—this has been achieved in recent years in the Cameroons: not only are the numbers of patients who attend the hospitals and dispensaries growing rapidly, but more Africans are receiving medical training and are qualifying for posts under the Administration, particularly in preventive medicine. In the Cameroons Province there are five hospitals for Africans, with rest-houses for the out-patients. In 1937, 4,486 in-patients and 35,747 out-patients received attention here. In addition there are thirteen Government dispensaries, numerous Mission dispensaries and travelling clinics. In 1937 the attendance at the Government dispensaries reached the figure of 173,787, an increase of 40,000 on the previous year. There is a child-welfare centre at Kake, and the Roman Catholic Mission maintains a maternity hospital at Kumbo where 220 babies were born in 1937, of whom only one died.

In the northern provinces of Kentu, Adamawa, and Dikwa, which are served only by dispensaries, the situation is not so satisfactory. It is heartening, however, to find the natives themselves demanding increased medical services. The most frequent diseases are those common to most tropical African countries —yaws, leprosy, malaria, and sleeping-sickness; meningitis (in Adamawa), small-pox, and chicken-pox. Perhaps the greatest improvements are to be hoped for from the spread of a knowledge of preventive medicine and sanitary precautions. Fortunately this is on the increase and is an important consequence of the development of education.

VII

If much still remains to be done in the British Cameroons, at least it can be said that it will have to be done along the lines of present policy. The policy may need more rapid and effective development, but it does not need redirection towards different ends. Perhaps the most substantial criticism of the present administration is its tendency to neglect the northern area and to concentrate upon the development of the Cameroons Province. One very good reason for this is the difficulty of communications inland: there are as yet no railways in the British Cameroons, and inevitably much more progress economically and socially has been made in the more accessible coastal districts. It is to be hoped that in time much more attention will be paid to the northern provinces.

In Nigeria and the British Cameroons an experiment has been begun which cannot be lightly abandoned. In the mandated territory the British Government is responsible for the lives of 800,000 natives, whose confidence and co-operation it has sought and in part won. To hand over these people to another Power, to treat them and their territory as no more than pawns in the game of international politics, to throw away all that has been slowly and patiently gained in the last twenty years, is to deny all sense of responsibility and obligation. The return of the British Cameroons to Germany would be of but slight value to the German people; it might well prove a disaster to the native population. Believing that it is the interests of the latter which should be placed above any considerations of prestige or any urge to national expansion, even though born of a divine mission, we unhesitatingly conclude against the return of this territory to Germany.

VIII

CONCLUSION

(*By* PROFESSOR VINCENT HARLOW)

WHEN a Great Power has been decisively defeated in the most terrible war that the world has yet known, and at the end of it proclaims that some of her property has been stolen by means of a confidence trick and demands its peaceful return as a matter of *right*, it is evident that a unique situation has arisen in international affairs. History, in modern as in ancient times, records examples of a foe having been induced, while still capable of resistance, to lay down his arms in expectation of more generous terms than he in fact received. That Germany was not in such a case in 1918 is proved by the insistence of Hindenburg and Ludendorff upon an immediate armistice at any cost. The German claim to a legal right in her former colonies will not bear examination.

And yet with growing vigour Germany maintains her demand for restitution, not only on grounds of legality, but of equity and natural justice; and Englishmen continue to ponder the proposition, write books about it, and engage in earnest discussion in the press. Clearly then something happened at the distribution of the spoil on this occasion—the introduction of some strange new value in international conduct, unknown to the diplomacy of previous generations. It did not, for example, occur to France

Conclusion

after the Peace of Paris in 1763 to bombard the Government of George III for the peaceful return of Canada on the plea that it was hers *jure divino*. Instead, she vowed vengeance and assisted in the disruption of the First British Empire. But it did—and does— occur to Germany in the twentieth century to make that novel plea. Is the reason to be found in a peculiar subtlety of the Teutonic mind, or did the victors—to their own embarrassment—furnish the cue?

At the peace settlement of 1919 a conflict of ideas arose with regard to colonial possessions which was the outward and visible sign of a profound change in important sections of the English-speaking world in relation to what is known as 'imperialism'. The reaction of British opinion to the Indian Mutiny and to the scramble for African and Pacific territories (which threatened the markets of a free-trade nation) provoked a revolt against the *laisser aller* attitude of the Manchester School, which took two forms. On the one hand, it produced the jingo, who set forth to confer the boon of anglicization upon a presumably grateful world. On the other hand, the liberal imperialist emerged, who disliked intensely the ὕβρις of his opposite number, was distrustful of the economic penetration which he witnessed overseas, and yet remained deeply convinced that the *Pax Britannica*, founded on principles of freedom and fair dealing, was a glorious conception, which if kept unsullied by greed and aggression could be the means of leading mankind to a better way of life. He was, in fact, the successor of the free-trade humanitarian of the middle decades of the century. Other sensitive minds, watching the disintegrating effects of European industrialism upon hapless peoples in Africa, Asia, and the Pacific, began to adhere to the new socialist doctrine that modern imperialism (as distinct from free settlement in empty, or comparatively empty, areas) was an inevitable and the most vicious emanation of the capitalist order. The salvation of the British worker and the helpless Kaffir could alone be achieved by the destruction, gradual or immediate, of capitalism and of the British Empire with it.

The effect of the South African War upon a community which included men of such diverse views was revolutionary. It was easy to be furious with the Kaiser for his impertinent, though comparatively innocuous, telegram to Kruger after the Jameson Raid: the explosion of feeling made men feel the better for it. But the cold disapproval of the other Powers when the war followed stung their pride. For the first time since Burke and Fox had defended the cause of the American rebels patriotism was not enough. Those who cheered a British defeat as a victory for freedom were a small minority; but a far greater number pondered deeply and with disturbed minds the implications of mining development on the Rand. The Treaty of Vereeniging, the rapid grants of internal self-government to the Transvaal and the Orange River Colony, culminating in the creation of an Anglo-Afrikaner Union of South Africa, justifiably

Conclusion

restored confidence in the constitutional principles of Durham and Elgin. But the problem of holding the balance between the interests of the native and the claims of the acquisitive white man was left unsolved. In fact, the principle of trusteeship in relation to the native was abandoned in South Africa (apart from the Protectorates) for the sake of meeting the challenge of white self-determination. Altogether, it had been a searing experience. The complacent exuberance of the last decades departed with the close of the century.

Thirteen uneasy years of growing tension in Europe ushered in the Great War. When virtually the whole of the civilized world became involved, political institutions of every kind and the established concepts upon which they had been built were subjected to the most searching test that human beings are able to apply. What in effect was worth fighting for and, if necessary, dying for, and what was not? The *status quo* in the body politic and in the individual mind was dissolved in the consuming heat of world war. It is needless to recapitulate the transformations in human society that resulted in Europe, in the Near and Far East; but it is important for our present purpose to note the process of revaluation in the minds of our own countrymen. The potent effect of propaganda upon an enemy is a familiar theme, but less attention has been devoted to its influence upon the propagandists themselves. From the British point of view entry into the war was an act of self-preservation. But as its casualties mounted and everything was put to the hazard, the immensity of the sacrifice called for a commensurate achievement. A war of protection against the domination of Imperial Germany—essentially similar, it was thought, to the preceding struggle with Napoleonic France—came to be regarded as 'a war to end war'. The triumph of national interests was an insufficient end to warrant such carnage and suffering. Nothing less would suffice than the establishment of a new world order that would make a repetition of the nightmare for ever impossible. From that it followed that an entirely new type of peace settlement was necessary.

Such was the conviction of a considerable body of opinion in this country. The application of these principles to the problem of imperialism induced a similar reaction. The attitude of mind which had rejected monopoly and territorial acquisition in the middle decades of the nineteenth century and which had wrestled in the post-1870 period with the uglier aspects of expansion among the coloured races was powerfully reinforced during the years of war. The *Round Table* group, leaders of the Labour party, and prominent publicists of varying political persuasions led a campaign to replace aggressive nationalist imperialism with a doctrine of trusteeship that would harmonize with the central concept of an international comity, designed to draw the teeth and pare the talons of nationalism itself. Similar ideas were widely held in the United States of America, and with an

Conclusion

assurance made possible by detachment, which was born of security.

On the other hand, the suffering of those four years coupled with the realization that the Allies had come near to breaking-point themselves before victory was achieved, produced precisely the opposite effect among a great number (possibly the majority) of Englishmen and almost all Frenchmen. A repetition of the ordeal must be avoided, not by reliance upon a new international ethic, but by such a weakening of Germany as would render her incapable of harm for the future. Safety for Rome by a Carthaginian peace. The issue was fairly joined.

And so the American President enunciated his famous fourteen principles and Clemenceau muttered that *le bon Dieu* had contented Himself with ten. If indeed a war-ridden generation could have risen above the standard of the Decalogue to that of the Sermon on the Mount, wisdom would have been justified of her children. As it was, most men (and therefore most politicians) compromised between the alternatives of security by force and security by moral suasion. Under the old dispensation Germany, having been defeated, could be reduced to the ranks—and she was: under the new she was admitted to membership of League, in which it was wicked to fight. The conflict of motives in the proceeding was for the most part unconscious: it represented a violent effort on the part of Christendom to haul itself up to a higher level while cautiously attempting to maintain contact with the lower rung. To adopt a somewhat different metaphor, the League developed rickets because it had for a wet-nurse the Treaty of Versailles.

The colonial settlement presented exactly similar features. President Wilson had promised in his Fifth Point that colonial claims would be adjusted by an open-minded consideration of the question of ownership on the one side, and the interests of the populations concerned on the other: and in a commentary on the Fourteen Points, approved by Wilson himself and subsequently published by Colonel House, the Fifth Point was interpreted to mean that the colonies would not be returned to Germany, but that the Power in whom control was vested must act as trustee for the natives under the League.[1]

Fear of Germany's declared designs for a *Mittel Afrika* and of the threat to Pacific communications brought France and the British Dominions to the Conference determined upon annexation as the time-honoured remedy to which they were legally entitled. There they were met by the counter-proposition that native territories were not property to be bandied about at a diplomatic fair, but a sacred trust. The resulting settlement by graded mandates was designed to serve the ends of security and trusteeship at one and the same time. The former was legitimate and the latter was noble, but they could not be combined in one system without mutual injury. Even a C Mandate over South

[1] Cf. above, p. 25.

Conclusion

West Africa did not provide the Union (as she is ruefully aware) with the same degree of security as outright annexation would have done. Similarly, the serious dilution of trusteeship which that type of mandate represents detracts from the moral strength of the system as a whole. Just as the traditional employment of overwhelming force in the Treaty of Versailles vitiated the Covenant of the League, so did the allocation of mandates by the Allied Powers among themselves under conditions designed to favour self-regarding interests invite an unjustified charge of cynical hypocrisy over the entire business.

A new principle of the highest importance in the relations between civilized and primitive peoples had been internationally proclaimed and adopted. But because it was impossible under the circumstances entirely to ignore national interests, the Allied Powers made the mistake of trying to justify acts done under the old dispensation in terms of the new. Hence it was that Germany was placed under the stigma of being judged incapable of ruling colonies because of previous mismanagement—a new principle; whereas the actual reason for rejecting her claims was the familiar and traditional one—that they dared not trust her as a neighbour. In the light of *ex post facto* wisdom it may be thought that the Allied Powers would have been better advised if they had refrained from taking the mandates for themselves. Their own security would have been substantially guaranteed if Tanganyika had been entrusted, for example, to Belgium and

South West Africa (as a B and not a C Mandate) had been consigned to Holland, an experienced Colonial Power with racial affinities with both Germans and Afrikaners. Yet, when all is said, the Allied Powers were fully entitled to retain what they had won by conquest since Germany had surrendered unconditionally, and they frankly explained that the primary reason for retention was regard for their own safety. If they then chose to administer the territories upon a new and better basis, that was their affair and to their credit. If they could have risen to a still higher level and could have brought themselves to trust their ex-enemy by including her as a partner in the new system, it would have been even more to their credit—indeed a gesture unique in the world's history. If their practice has fallen short in some respects of their original professions, no injury has been inflicted thereby upon the former owner: and the fact remains that the Mandate system with all its concessions to Mammon has gone far in securing a nobler tradition in the administration of backward peoples. Germany has two legitimate grievances in the matter, and two only: that the capital value of her former colonies was not taken into account in the assessment of reparations, and that the Allies were gratuitously offensive in putting forward a moral reason for their refusal to associate her with themselves in the new experiment.

The latter point does not, however, constitute a grievance in the form put forward by German propagandists. To indict Germany as a nation unfit by its

Conclusion

record to be trusted with the administration of native races was gratuitous and unnecessary, for the (declared) motive of excluding German military ambition from Africa and the Pacific was both legitimate and sufficient in itself. But a gratuitous act is not necessarily a lie. There is unimpeachable evidence to show that Germany's colonial record consisted of twenty years of thoroughly bad administration, followed by seven years of great improvement, which by accepted standards still left much to be desired. Germany was excluded, primarily, because the exhausted victors felt that she would be dangerous, and, secondarily, because she was thought to be unsuitable. The second reason—though sincerely held—should have been omitted. An impregnable case was gratuitously weakened by its inclusion and still more so by exaggeration in its presentation. It was as though a headmaster had dismissed a member of his staff, publicly explaining that the offender was undermining his authority and was also addicted to bullying the boys, the latter charge being substantially true, but one which under other circumstances would not have been ventilated.

From the evidence adduced in a previous section of this book it is clear that the American President did not contemplate the return of the colonies to Germany as sovereign property. The question to be considered was whether the interests of the subject races would be best served by being placed under German trusteeship or by some other means. But the conception of trusteeship on behalf of an international organization is one that the present régime of the German Reich utterly and contemptuously rejects. In other words, the German Government appeals to the American President's exposition of international idealism as justification for a claim to possessive sovereignty over alien races. She cannot, one would think, have it both ways. If the argument is that she laid down her arms in the confident expectation that the disposition of her colonial territories would be the subject of investigation and negotiation and that she would otherwise have continued the war, the facts, as has been shown, are against the contention. If, on the other hand, she accepts the implications of Wilson's programme, she must re-enter the League, sincerely adhere to the terms of the Covenant, and then demand a place among the Mandatory Powers. In that event there would be many in this country who would feel that the claim should be met and, furthermore, that the other European Powers should at the same time accept a similar supervision in respect of their own coloured dependencies. But no such action is contemplated by Germany, nor indeed is it conceivable that it would be. The Nazi philosophy is the negation of any form of internationalism.

The argument advanced by German publicists (and by Herr Hitler himself in his speech before the Reichstag in February 1939) that the restoration of the colonies would make a substantial contribution towards a solution of Germany's economic difficulties is very adequately dealt with in a previous section and calls for little further comment. Eighty-five per cent. of the raw materials which Germany is obliged to import can be obtained only from independent states. Whether the 1 per cent. imported from her colonies in pre-War days could be raised to 15 per cent., as is claimed, is a matter of conjecture. In 1934 out of a total import of 1,045 million gold dollars the former colonies contributed 2·9 million dollars.[1] But even if the maximum figure was reached by monopoly and intensive development, it would probably be at the cost of severe financial strain during the process. The point is well put by Dr. M. J. Bonn:

'Non-German capital at present invested in the mandates might wish to retire when a new administration came in; whether or not some sort of compensation were to be paid, Germany's foreign debts would increase. If foreign capitalists did not withdraw their participations, a large part of the profits earned by them would go abroad in return for the money invested by them. Whilst Germany might draw her supplies from the Colonies, part of the payments made for them would flow to foreign countries. Preferential treatment in German markets would benefit these foreign investors and raise the costs of raw materials to the German producer. The stimulus given to the production of additional goods would inflate the world's supply of raw materials, for world markets are already overstocked; world prices might fall and Germany's commercial rivals would get raw materials more cheaply than she. At the same time, the foreign

[1] The total production of these territories in that year was 26·5 million dollars.

colonial producers' purchasing power for industrial goods might decline, and with it Germany's foreign trade.'[1]

Moreover, the usefulness of these territories as a source of supply in war (the chief preoccupation of the German Government) would disappear unless communications could be kept open by superiority of sea power.

Members of the Group were agreed that if Germany, in the pursuit of political objectives, chose to erect a closed economic system, which caused her to experience difficulties in buying raw materials in the world market, the remedy in the first instance lay with herself. Moreover, while the extension of autarchy to Africa was of doubtful value to Germany and still less to world trade as a whole, it was also agreed that preferential tariffs and quotas applied by other Powers to their colonial dependencies, in that they restricted the commercial opportunities of non-colonial Powers, were unfair and should be removed. In a world in which all the colonial territories put together contribute only 3 per cent. of the total supply of raw materials and foodstuffs, the proposition that intensive methods in certain of those areas could appreciably alter the balance appeared to be untenable. Yet Germany was insistent upon her determination and her right to make the experiment. This circumstance led to a very thorough discussion on the probable effects upon the native population.

The discussion emphasized the antithesis that exists between the British and the South African point

[1] *The Crumbling of Empire*, Allen & Unwin, 1938, p. 387.

Conclusion

of view in regard to native administration. The United Kingdom representatives and most of those from other Dominions upheld the view that the true interests of the native cannot be maintained in the presence of intensive commercial exploitation, which disintegrates tribal life and promotes material prosperity at the expense of social values. The policy of shielding the native against such corrosive penetration, which had been adopted in Nigeria, Tanganyika, and elsewhere, had, it was maintained, been richly justified by experience. Insulation in such areas had made it possible, through the system known as Indirect Rule, to begin to train the native to become a self-reliant African instead of a de-racialized imitation of the white man. Why should this fruitful experiment—of the utmost significance for the future of Africa—be abandoned in Tanganyika and the Cameroons for the sake of a commercial development, the harmful effects of which were certain and the benefits to the exploiter comparatively insubstantial?

The South African view was different. They held (accurately representing their countrymen) that the egalitarian objective in respect of the Africans was false and unreal. The only sound method by which he could be trained up to a civilized level was to construct in his midst a strongly developed European society, preserved as such by means of social and economic differentiation. Work for the African in field and mine maintained that society, while at the same time bringing the labourer into contact with civilized standards. This method, combined with an enlightened administration of native locations, was the only reliable way to develop the African, because it accepted him as he really was and did not act upon an unjustified assumption of potentialities.

Those who upheld this policy accordingly discounted the injury alleged by others to be the inevitable outcome of a German Four Years' Plan in the restored territories. Indeed, some South Africans were not unfavourable to the re-entry of Germany into the African Continent. It might appease a dangerously discontented Power, whose doctrine of racial exclusiveness had much in common with their own. Germany might well prove a useful neighbour, but at a safe distance. South West Africa was too close: so, too, was Tanganyika.

The general opinion, however, was that the establishment of the principles of mandatory rule in Tanganyika, the Cameroons, and (to a less but still substantial extent) in South West Africa was an enormous moral gain which, instead of being lost, should be consolidated and extended.

The long and earnest discussions that took place week by week on the reports which had been prepared on the various aspects of this subject are described in this book in a compressed and summarized form. It was obviously impossible to reproduce the testing and probing that went on in debate. One impression, however, may be permitted. Most, if not all, of those who took part began with a sincere hope and desire

Conclusion

that 'something could be done' to meet the German claims. As the investigation proceeded from questions of legal right, through economic need, to problems of native welfare and considerations of security, a gradual stiffening of attitude became apparent. The participants felt themselves compelled in considering charges of deceit and hypocrisy to examine as candidly and as honestly as they could the motivations of the 'imperialism' of the various member states of the British Commonwealth which they represented. Two considerations became dominant in their minds: could the territories be restored without seriously endangering the safety of the restorers, and ought it to be done in view of the majority's conception of native welfare?

To the first question the eventual answer was a reluctant but decisive negative. Germany, in fact, was demanding that the British Empire should of her own volition weaken her strategic resources at a time of grave national peril, when the military power of Germany had become supreme in central Europe, when the preponderance of her air force threatened the existence of London and other ports vital for food supply, and when her association with Italy and Japan would put an almost intolerable strain upon Britain's defence of oceanic communications in the event of war. Serious consideration was given to the proposition that if the policy of appeasement was extended to include concession in the colonial sphere, the only question at issue between Germany and the

British Empire would be resolved and a long step taken towards a general pacification. On the face of it, the proposition seemed attractive. A fuller examination, however, brought home the point that the existing pressure upon the existing democracies was world-wide. To weaken the defensive front in Africa and the Pacific would not only give rise to serious difficulties in intra-Commonwealth relations, but also jeopardize Britain's powers of resistance if she became involved (by way of Tunisia, for example) in defending the Channel ports.

Owing to the policy adopted by the totalitarian Powers it is impossible to treat the Anglo-German colonial controversy in its strategical aspects in isolation. The history of Germany's recent relations with the Czechs has all too aptly illustrated the truth of the proverb, *l'appétit vient en mangeant*.

On the moral issue concerning the native populations, the conclusion of the majority was no less emphatic. While frankly recognizing the marked improvement in German administration during the seven years preceding the Great War, it was recalled that reform had been initiated under the pressure of liberal and socialist criticism, which to-day was dumb.

No one took pleasure in reaching these negative conclusions. It was realized that behind all the dialectical arguments advanced by General von Epp and his associates the real driving force was a sense of impaired prestige and injured *amour propre*. 'The white man's burden', so ridiculed a generation ago

Conclusion 213

as a hypocritical cloak for greed, has now become a badge of rank, and all the more so because it is already worn by every other nation aspiring to be recognized as a Great Power. Credits and free access to raw materials and markets in the colonial dependencies of other Powers are sops which do not touch the central issue and which Germany proudly ignores, biding her opportunity. Colonies, we are told, are are not 'a matter for mobilization': in the fullness of time they may be.

To-day there is no outlet overseas for Germany's frustrated ambition: all the areas where European control is practicable have already been allotted. She can only shoulder her way in again at the expense of others. Yet the members of this Group became convinced that for our own safety we could not facilitate that re-entry, and that furthermore we ought not to hand over the future of primitive races to a régime whose principles and standards were fundamentally opposed to our own.

Is there then no resolving of the dilemma? Must we continue indefinitely—or so long as we are able—to thwart German imperial ambitions beyond the seas? Time was when this country (often very willingly) made room for Germany, and France too, in Africa and among the Pacific islands. But that was in the days when the Royal Navy was supreme in the Seven Seas and no serious threat to our security was involved. The policy cannot be repeated, except, indeed, in the unlikely contingency of the ice-cap receding in Antarctica. As in the case of the United States of America, the world's colonial frontier has reached the limit and ceased to move. If there are to be further adjustments, that which is available must be shared. And yet the members of this Group have come to the conclusion that under the conditions in which we are living the British Empire cannot and must not yield up her responsibilities.

One way remains for this and for other world issues —the abandonment by all concerned of the outworn conception of national sovereignty: the pooling of resources, of commercial opportunities, and moral responsibilities. But that is a vision that finds no response in a Germany which claims sole ownership of the soil and people of certain regions for her own purposes and to the detriment of others. If and when confidence and trust sufficiently revive to make it possible to place the African Continent in the care of an all-embracing trusteeship, the initiative must come from us in an invitation to Germany to take her part. But co-operation on such terms is possible only with a German régime that has not yet been born.

APPENDIX I

I. NEW GUINEA

THE island of New Guinea was first discovered by European explorers in the sixteenth century. In the late eighteenth and early nineteenth centuries both the Dutch and the English established forts and trading stations on the island. There was a rough division into a western, Dutch sphere of influence, and an eastern, British sphere. In the second half of the nineteenth century German traders became active in the South Pacific, and in 1882 these traders pressed the German Government to annex at least part of the Territory. The dangers of foreign occupation were felt keenly by the Queensland Government, which urged Mr. Gladstone's Government in Great Britain to forestall possible German annexation. Gladstone, however, refused and disavowed the action of Queensland in seizing the mainland opposite her own shores.

The next step was taken by the German Government of Bismarck, which in 1884 annexed the north-east coast and the adjacent islands. In a belated attempt to prevent further German expansion, Commodore Erskine, with the approval of the British Government, proclaimed a British Protectorate over the south-east quarter of the island, and in 1885 a boundary agreement was reached between the two Powers. By this the Dutch claims to the western half were recognized. Germany secured the northern portion of New Guinea (known as Kaiser Wilhelmsland), all the islands off the north coast, and the New Britain group of islands.

In 1888 the British Protectorate became a dependency controlled by Queensland and in 1906 was re-named the

Territory of Papua. In 1889 the German New Guinea Company, which had hitherto controlled the development of the German Colony, surrendered their charter and the Imperial Government assumed direct administration.

The fundamental obstacle to the development of New Guinea has always been the difficulty of penetrating inland beyond the narrow coastal areas. The interior of the island is dominated by great ranges of mountains, rising to heights of 10,000–15,000 feet. The Germans made little attempt to open up the Hinterland. They were content to develop the coastal region and the islands. Here they built roads and a port at Blanche Bay. Kopoko was the first capital, but the administrative centre was later moved to Rabaul on the island of New Britain. The history of the German occupation was uneventful. Trade was their supreme object and the island's wealth in copra was developed by the system of *Kiap*, or Government plantations. The climate of New Guinea is not favourable to European settlement—there were under a thousand whites in the territory of the islands—and to supplement the native supply of labour the Germans encouraged Asiatic immigration. Very little evidence is available as to the character of German rule, but there are no grounds for believing that it was unduly oppressive.

On the outbreak of war in 1914 the Australian Government at once undertook the reduction of the Territory by an expeditionary force, and from 1914 to 1921 the country was under military administration. After the peace settlement Australia obtained a mandate for the former German colony and since 1921 a civil administration, distinct from that of Papua, has been established at Rabaul.

Appendix I

Australia—after her failure at the Peace Conference to secure annexation—accepted the obligation of a 'C' Mandate for New Guinea. These obligations do not include the 'Open Door', as do the 'B' Mandates in Africa. Administration is in the hands of a Governor-General who governs by decree, subject to the Commonwealth Government's veto. The principal concern of the Administration for some years was to explore and to establish contact with the inland districts. The geographical difficulties of such work has already been mentioned; to these were added the hostility and suspicion of a primitive people with traditions of intertribal warfare and head-hunting expeditions. The magnificent work of the District Field Staffs has done a great deal to overcome these obstacles and to open up the hitherto inaccessible Hinterland.

The discovery of gold in the Moroke District in 1926 forced the Administration to abandon its plans for gradual development. An effective solution to the new problems of transport and communication was found in the use of the aeroplane, despite the difficulties of flying and landing in so mountainous a country.

The production of gold has continued to increase and in 1937 the export of gold reached nearly £2,000,000 in value. The territory is believed to possess other valuable mineral resources; in particular, the possibilities of New Guinea's oil supplies in the Sepik District are being explored.

Despite its mineral wealth, the prosperity of New Guinea must depend ultimately on its agricultural development. The Germans during their occupation did not exercise sufficient care in the alienation of native lands. Large areas were sold to planters, who in many cases dispossessed natives, with disastrous results.

Although no figures can be quoted, it is plausible to suppose that the decrease in population was coincident with, and consequent upon, the loss of planting lands. Now, as then—apart from foods produced for native consumption—the agriculture of the Territory is dominated by one product, copra. But much of the territory is unsuited to the coco-nut palm, which only grows near salt water, and efforts have therefore been made to supplement the copra production with cocoa, tobacco, coffee, tea, cotton, kapok, oil, rubber, spices, and tropical fruits. Plant nurseries, experimental stations, and meteorological observatories have been established and inspectors appointed to deal with pests and diseases, and to instruct the natives in better methods of cultivation.

Since 1928 the agricultural policy of the Administration has been to encourage the cultivation of a suitable cereal crop, not least in order to meet the deficiencies of the native diet.

The aim of the Administration is to develop native cultivation. In 1937 there were 462 plantations in the territory, covering an area of 197,230 hectares, with 98,447 hectares under cultivation.

But the vital problem which confronts the present Administration is that of population. The climate is not suitable for intensive white settlement, and the territory is sparsely populated by natives. The labour supply is insufficient for a thorough economic development of the Territory, yet the Administration has refused, in the interests of the native peoples, to permit Asiatic immigration. There is in fact a small Chinese community on the island, settled there since the time of the German occupation. The demand has been heard that the former German policy of encouraging Asiatic immigration should be revived, but up to the present time the Administration

Appendix I

has refused to adopt it. The problem of under-population, however, remains, and is likely to become more serious. It is indeed possible that the Government may eventually have to face a choice between the exploitation of the Territory's resources and the continuation of the present safeguards for the natives' welfare at the cost of retarded economic development.

The possible strategic threat to Australia from a hostile power's possession of New Guinea is not difficult to see. Geographically it is well placed as a base for attacks by air or sea upon the coast of Queensland and New South Wales. Whether advantage could be taken of its geographical position is more difficult to say. The answer to that question must depend very much upon the naval strength of the British Empire and of the forces available at Singapore, the strategic key to the whole of this area. Australia, however, is very averse from taking the risk and would be hostile to any suggestion of return. This fact would be of great importance, should the proposal for the return of the ex-German colonies ever be put forward in definite form. Evidently the British Government would have to take careful consideration of the Australian attitude; and that has been put very succinctly by Sir George Pearce, the Minister for External Affairs, when he said in 1936: 'The return of the territories under Australian Mandate is unthinkable.'

II. WEST SAMOA

The Archipelago of Samoa lies in the South Pacific and consists of fourteen islands of which eight—Savaii, Manoro, Apolima, Upolu, Fanuatapu, Manua, Nuutele, and Nuulua—form the political unit of West Samoa. It is a well favoured country, with abundant rainfall, an igneous soil of great fertility, and wide tracts of forest.

Appendix I

Most of the islands are considerably elevated, with several extinct volcanic craters rising from 2,000 to 4,000 feet. They are inhabited by the Samoans, a Polynesian race of fine physique, with a well-developed social life.

In the middle of the nineteenth century, British, German, and American traders began to frequent Samoa, and in 1889, as a result of the continued intertribal wars, a protectorate was set up by these three Powers. This arrangement proved unsatisfactory; the native wars continued and the rivalry of British and German traders became intense. In 1900 a fresh settlement was reached by which Great Britain, in return for compensation elsewhere, withdrew from Samoa altogether. The islands were then divided between Germany and America, Germany keeping the western islands.

The fourteen years of German administration were by no means undisturbed, but the Germans showed considerable tact in handling their problems. On taking over the Government, they set out to make use of the existing Samoan institutions, nominated native administrators on the old native family basis of control, and retained the paramount Samoan chief in his position. By 1904, however, it became apparent that the system was likely to prove a failure.

In that year a 'Samoa for the Samoans' movement, led by the German-nominated native administrators, arose. This, like all troubles during the German period of control, was firmly put down, and in 1905 these administrators were abolished and the old Samoan family relationships abandoned as an administrative basis. The *Fono a Faipule* was set up, an advisory council based on districts, paid and appointed by the Government. In 1909 there were large-scale attempts to restore the native administration and large bodies of natives assembled to enforce their demands. This movement was put down by force with the assistance of warships from the German China station; and there was a tightening up of discipline in general. In 1912 the paramount chief died and two claimants appeared. The Germans tactfully appointed both to a newly created position. The feeling, however, became very strong that the *Fono* were mere Government tools, and the administration became more and more a 'strong-hand' control, which was maintained until, on the outbreak of war in 1914, the New Zealand Expeditionary Force took over.

After the peace settlement Western Samoa came under the administration of New Zealand as a 'C' Mandate. The inexperience of the Administration in the early years did little to lessen its difficulties. The Samoans showed considerable hostility to any attempt to disturb their traditional ways of life. They are a conservative people with a love for elaborate ceremonial and time-honoured customs. Indirect rule is made difficult because the Samoan chief considers the details of administrative work beneath his dignity and occupies himself in the more congenial ways of political intrigue and long, general discussions. The chiefs showed little sympathy with the Administration's enthusiastic and over-optimistic schemes for an improved system of Government.

There has been equal hostility to attempts at economic development. The native economic system appears to have been based upon the principle of 'least effort'. It was a communal system, in which the members of a family group supported each other, and it was totally opposed to European ideas of efficiency and maximum production. The Samoans live in a fertile country where little labour is required to support life, and they do not take kindly to the idea of intensive work. The difficulty of securing an adequate labour-supply, without using political and economic pressure and forcing the native to work, therefore prevents the full development of the tropical fertility of the islands.

At all periods of Samoan history the European traders have complained that they are unable to extract a fair profit owing to the 'absurd' regulations of the Government. On the whole the Administration has done its best to protect the interests of the natives against exploitation by the traders and capitalists. The opposition of the European and Asiatic trading classes has, however, considerably hampered the work of Government. They are constantly pressing for the diminution of the power of the Administrator and for a more democratic form of government, although the Administration claim that this would simply mean the exploitation of the natives, who do not understand and would take no advantage of Western institutions.

Resistance to the Administration's policy came to a head in the *Mau* agitation, which involved at one time more than half the islanders in a general passive resistance to the Government. The movement was fomented by European traders just after the Administration had inaugurated a scheme to protect the native by arranging for the marketing of his copra—a measure, incidentally, which raised considerably the quality produced by the natives' private enterprise. The agitation was not dealt with wisely: a Royal Commission, which investigated the affair from a narrow legalistic point of view, failed to appreciate the genuine grievances of the natives and regarded the disturbance merely as a European intrigue. In the winter of 1929–30, three years after the outbreak of trouble, stronger measures had to be taken and the strength of the movement was broken.

With the advent of the Labour Party to power in New Zealand considerable changes in policy, in the interests of the natives, were made. In 1936 a goodwill mission was sent to Samoa from New Zealand and representation was granted to the Samoans on the Legislative Council and Finance Committee. The Council of the chiefs (*Faipules*) was re-elected and 33 of its 39 members had been members of the *Mau*. Co-operation has thus been ensured for the time being and the long struggle ended.

From a strategic point of view there is little to be said. Samoa is 1,300 miles away from New Zealand and the only good base—Pago-Pago—lies in East Samoa and has already been utilized by the U.S.A.

Economically, West Samoa is prosperous; her exports of copra, cocoa, and bananas continue to increase. The majority of her trade is with British countries—the United Kingdom, Australia, and New Zealand. The question of return to Germany has never become a vital issue in Samoa, as it has in South West Africa or Tanganyika, but it is unquestionable that New Zealand, which has encountered most of its difficulties in an attempt to carry out the provisions of the Mandate and to safeguard the interests of the native population, would be very reluctant to surrender her Mandate from the League.

III. NAURU

Nauru is a small Pacific island situated 26 miles south of the Equator in longitude 166 degrees East. Its area of 8 square miles supports, according to the latest estimate, 2,696 people. On 1 October 1888 the island became German territory and it remained under the administration of the German Marshall Islands Group until its surrender to the Australian forces in 1914.

Nauru is a peculiar case in the 'C' group of mandates,

for it is a mandate not of Great Britain or of a particular Dominion, but of the British Empire as a whole. For practical purposes, however, the administration of the island was vested in the Governments of Australia and New Zealand (by virtue of their geographical position) and of the United Kingdom. These three Governments agreed on 2 July 1919 that the island should be placed under an Administrator to be appointed in the first instance by Australia. Since then Australia has become the *de facto* administrator of Nauru.

The Administrator has all the executive, legislative, and judicial powers of government, and is responsible for the material, moral, and social welfare of all the inhabitants of the island. The island is divided into fourteen districts each headed by an elected Chief, the fourteen Chiefs being under a Head Chief and his Deputy. The Chief is responsible for the maintenance of order in his district and, subject to appeal to the Administrator, is empowered to deal with minor offences.

In the administration of the island, native interests are represented by an Advisory Council consisting of the Head Chief, the Deputy Head Chief, and the Chiefs elected by the natives from each of the fourteen districts. The interests of the Chinese labour force are represented by a liaison officer between the Chinese community and the Administrator, and the senior executive officers of the British Phosphates Commission represent the island's industry and the European group.

In a classification of colonial territory with respect to the kind of advantage offered, Nauru would be placed as a supplier of raw material. The island's claim to significance is its rich deposits of phosphate. In 1934 colonial production accounted for 52 per cent. of the world's commercial production of phosphate. The principal sources of this colonial commercial production of phosphate (their production being expressed as a percentage of world commercial production) were: French North Africa 34·6 per cent.; French equatorial Africa 7·2 per cent.; Nauru 4·5 per cent. (net exports). Thus the export of phosphate constitutes practically the whole of Nauruan commercial activity. Copra is exported in comparatively negligible quantities.

The mining rights are vested in the British Phosphates Commission, which is, in effect, a monopoly. In 1905 the original German company, the *Jaluit Gesellschaft*, sold its rights to exploit the phosphate deposits to the Pacific Phosphates Company, a company registered in Great Britain. In addition to the Nauru deposits, the Pacific Phosphates Company also obtained a concession to work the deposits in the adjacent British territory of Ocean Island. In 1919 the British, Australian, and New Zealand Governments acquired by purchase from the Pacific Phosphates Company the exclusive rights to work these deposits. These Governments vested their interests in the British Phosphates Commission. Although it is a semi-official body, the Commission operates as a private company with powers limited to the exploitation of the phosphate deposits.

Owing to the royalties paid by the British Phosphates Commission, Nauru is a very prosperous territory. All expenditure is met from local revenue. The island's exports have been largely confined to Australia and New Zealand and its imports have been chiefly from Australia. As in the case of the *Jaluit Gesellschaft* under the German régime, the Commission is granted freedom from import duties on certain articles.

Within this governmental and industrial framework the Administration has endeavoured to prevent exploitation of the native population and to encourage the preservation of native rights and customs. Forced labour in lieu of taxation, or for any purpose, even including public works, is not permitted. Nauruans may not be recruited for employment abroad. The labour force required for the mining of phosphate is chiefly Chinese, recruited by voluntary agreement under three-year contracts. The agreement, hours, wages, compensation, and conditions of labour are subject to the approval and supervision of the Administrator. The Nauruan native, generally speaking, is not disposed to any kind of sustained work and the employment which he prefers is of a casual nature and principally agricultural. The community of imported labour constitutes a market which absorbs his surplus food products.

An agreement between the natives and the British Phosphates Commission, which, from 1 July 1927, superseded the former plan of royalty and land payments, considerably benefited the natives. The payment to the natives by the Commission for phosphate land worked was increased from £20 to £40 per acre; the royalty paid by the Commission for a ton of exported phosphate was increased from $3d.$ to $7\frac{1}{2}d.$, of which $4d.$ was to be paid directly to the Nauruan landowner instead of the $2d.$ formerly paid, $1\frac{1}{2}d.$ instead of $1d.$ to the Administrator to be used solely for the benefit of the Nauruans; and $2d.$ to the Nauruan Royalty Trust Fund. This Fund was not to constitute part of the territory's budget but was to be ear-marked solely for native welfare.

With the exception of the small allotments held by the Government and the Missions, the whole of the island is owned by individual natives. The alienation of land in which natives exercise rights by virtue of use or heredity is governed by local native custom. However, to protect

Appendix I

'a simple-minded people not versed in land values', the Lands Ordinance of 1921 made it illegal for any agreement to be effected with respect to land unless the consent of the Government was first obtained.

Liberty of conscience and religion of the Nauruans and other residents of the island is preserved. Particular attention has also been paid to the education of the native population. By the Compulsory Education Ordinance of 1921 it is obligatory for children from 6 to 16 years of age to attend school; there is an additional vocational course for boys and girls, and continuation lectures for adults. The educational staff of the native schools is composed of Nauruans, and some attempt is being made to introduce Nuaruans into junior administrative posts.

APPENDIX II

MANDATES CONSTITUTIONS

WE quote the British Mandate for the British Cameroons as an example of a 'B' Mandate:

Article 1: Demarcation of the boundaries between the French and British Cameroons.

Article 2: 'The Mandatory shall be responsible for the peace, order, and good government of the territory, and for the promotion to the utmost of the material and moral well-being and the social progress of its inhabitants.

Article 3: 'The Mandatory shall not establish in the territory any military or naval bases, nor erect any fortifications, nor organize any native force, except for local police purposes and for the defence of the territory.

Article 4: 'The Mandatory:

(1) Shall provide for the eventual emancipation of all slaves, and for as speedy an elimination of domestic and other slavery as social conditions will allow:

(2) Shall suppress all forms of slave trade:

(3) Shall prohibit all forms of forced or compulsory labour, except for essential public works, and then only in return for adequate remuneration:

(4) Shall protect the natives from abuse and measures of fraud and force by the careful supervision of labour contracts and the recruiting of labour:

(5) Shall exercise a strict control over the traffic in arms and ammunition and the sale of spirituous liquors.

Article 5: 'In the framing of laws relating to the holding or transfer of land, the Mandatory shall take into consideration native laws and customs, and shall respect the rights and safeguard the interests of the native population.

'No native land may be transferred, except between

Appendix II

natives, without the previous consent of the public authorities, and no real rights over native land in favour of non-natives may be created except with the same consent.

'The Mandatory shall promulgate strict regulations against usury.

Article 6: 'The Mandatory shall secure to all nationals of States Members of the League of Nations the same rights as are enjoyed in the territory by his own nationals in respect of entry into and residence in the territory, the protection afforded to their person and property, and acquisition of property, movable and immovable, and the exercise of their profession or trade, subject only to the requirements of public order and on condition of compliance with the local law.

'Further, the Mandatory shall ensure to all States Members of the League of Nations on the same footing as to his own nationals, freedom of transit and navigation, and complete economic and industrial equality; except that the Mandatory shall be free to organize essential public works and services on such terms and conditions as he thinks just.

'Concessions for the development of the natural resources of the territory shall be granted by the Mandatory without distinction on grounds of nationality between the nationals of all States Members of the League of Nations, but on such conditions as will maintain intact the authority of the local government.

'Concessions having the character of a general monopoly shall not be granted. This provision does not affect the right of the Mandatory to create monopolies of a purely fiscal character in the interest of the territory under mandate and in order to provide the territory with fiscal resources which seem best suited to the local requirements;

or, in certain cases, to carry out the development of natural resources, either directly by the State or by a controlled agency, provided that there shall result therefrom no monopoly of the natural resources for the benefit of the Mandatory or his nationals, directly or indirectly, nor any preferential advantage which shall be inconsistent with the economic, commercial, and industrial equality hereinbefore guaranteed.

'The rights conferred by this article extend equally to companies and associations organized in accordance with the law of any of the States Members of the League of Nations, subject only to the requirements of public order, and on conditions of compliance with the local law.

Article 7: 'The Mandatory shall ensure in the territory complete freedom of conscience, and the free exercise of all forms of worship which are consonant with public order and morality: missionaries who are nationals of States Members of the League of Nations shall be free to enter the territory and to travel and reside therein, to acquire and possess property, to erect religious buildings, and to open schools throughout the territory; it being understood, however, that the Mandatory shall have the right to exercise such control as may be necessary for the maintenance of public order and good government, and to take all measures required for such control.

Article 8: 'The Mandatory shall apply to the territory any general international conventions applicable to his contiguous territory.

Article 9: 'The Mandatory shall have full powers of administration and legislation in the area subject to the mandate. This area shall be administered in accordance with the laws of the Mandatory as an integral part of his territory and subject to the above provisions.

'The Mandatory shall therefore be at liberty to apply

Appendix II

his laws to the territory under the mandate subject to the modifications required by local conditions, and to constitute the territory into a customs, fiscal, or administrative union or federation with the adjacent territories under his sovereignty or control, provided always that the measures adopted to that end do not infringe the provisions of this mandate.'

Articles 10, 11, and 12: The Mandatory is required to make an annual report to the Council of the League of Nations. The consent of the Council of the League is required for any modification of the mandate.

Disputes relating to the mandate which cannot be settled by negotiation are to be submitted to the Permanent Court of International Justice.

The British and French Cameroons, British and French Togoland, Ruanda-Urundi, and Tanganyika are held under 'B' Mandates. In the case of the French mandates, however, the following addition is made to Article 3:

'It is understood, however, that the troops thus raised may, in the event of general war, be utilised to repel an attack or for defence of the territory outside that subject to the mandate.'.

We quote the Mandate for the Union Government for South West Africa as an example of a 'C' Mandate.

Article 1: Definition of the Territory.

Article 2: 'The Mandatory shall have full power of administration and legislation over the territory subject to the present mandate as an integral portion of the Union of South Africa, and may apply the laws of the Union of South Africa to the territory, subject to such local modifications as circumstances may require.

'The Mandatory shall promote to the utmost the material and moral well-being and the social progress of the inhabitants of the territory subject to the present mandate.

Article 3: 'The Mandatory shall see that the slave-trade is prohibited, and that no forced labour is permitted, except for essential public works and services, and then only for adequate remuneration.

'The Mandatory shall also see that the traffic in arms and ammunition is controlled in accordance with principles analogous to those laid down in the convention relating to the control of the arms traffic, signed on the 10th September, 1919, or in any convention amending the same.

'The supply of intoxicating spirits and beverages to the natives shall be prohibited.

Article 4: 'The military training of the natives, otherwise than for purposes of internal police and the local defence of the territory, shall be prohibited. Furthermore, no military or naval bases shall be established or fortifications erected in the territory.

Article 5: 'Subject to the provisions of any local law for the maintenance of public order and public morals, the Mandatory shall ensure in the territory freedom of conscience and the free exercise of all forms of worship, and shall allow all missionaries, nationals of any State Member of the League of Nations, to enter into, travel, and reside in the territory for the purpose of prosecuting their calling.'

Articles 6 and 7: These correspond to Articles 10, 11, and 12 of the 'B' Mandates.

South West Africa, Samoa, Nauru, and New Guinea are all held under 'C' Mandates.

APPENDIX III

I. TRADE OF GERMAN COLONIES,[1]
1913–14

1. Trade of the German Colonies (1913–14).

Colony	Exports	Imports
	Marks	Marks
German E. Africa	31,418,000	50,309,000
German S.W. Africa	39,000,000	32,500,000
Kamerun	23,336,000	34,241,000
Togo	9,958,000	11,427,000
New Guinea (Kaiser Wilhelms land)	5,100,000	5,871,000
W. Samoa	5,100,000	4,900,000
Caroline, Pelew, and Marshall Is.	6,900,000	3,400,000
Kiauchow	79,640,000	6,062,700

2. Percentage of Germany's total consumption in raw materials and other products supplied by the Colonies in 1910. [Table in Otto Mayer, *Die Entwicklung der Handelsbeziehungen Deutschlands zu seinen Kolonien* (1913), p. 178, quoted by Henderson, op. cit., p. 16.]

Product	Quantity	Value
	(Per cent.)	(Per cent.)
Cotton	0·25	0·25
Rubber	13·62	12·33
Oils and fats	2·12	2·66
Tropical timber	4·07	3·43
Wool	0·03	0·02
Hides and skins	0·15	0·17
Wax	8·09	8·14
Ivory	6·06	6·09
Mica	6·21	6·31
Precious Stones	0·30	37·35

[1] For a full and detailed examination of Germany's trade with her colonies before the War, see W. O. Henderson in the *Economic History Review*, vol. ix. 1 (Nov. 1938), pp. 1–16.

Appendix III

3. Germany's commercial relations with her Colonies from 1900 to 1910 in relation to her total trade (in million marks). [Table in Otto Mayer, op. cit., quoted by Henderson, p. 16.]

Year	Total imports into Germany	Imports from Colonies	Percentage of Colonial imports	Total exports from Germany	Exports to Colonies	Percentage of Colonial exports
1900	6,320·4	6·5	0·10	4,893·8	23·3	0·48
1901	5,710·3	5·8	0·10	4,512·6	20·7	0·46
1902	5,805·8	6·9	0·12	4,812·8	21·1	0·44
1903	6,321·1	7·3	0·12	5,130·3	23·5	0·46
1904	6,854·5	11·1	0·16	5,315·6	33·1	0·62
1905	7,436·3	17·7	0·24	5,841·8	43·6	0·74
1906	8,438·6	20·3	0·24	6,475·6	43·0	0·67
1907	9,003·3	22·9	0·25	7,094·9	37·9	0·53
1908	8,077·1	21·9	0·27	6,481·5	36·5	0·56
1909	8,860·4	29·4	0·33	6,858·7	41·8	0·61
1910	9,310·0	50·1	0·54	7,644·2	55·6	0·73

II. TRADE OF BRITISH MANDATED TERRITORIES

(All figures, except those for Togoland, from the official Statistical Abstract for the British Empire, 1938)

1. Tanganyika.

	1935	1936	1937
	£	£	£
Total imports .	2,989,000	3,356,860	3,924,095
Total exports*	3,723,688	4,805,958	5,311,464
Chief exports:			
Sisal .	1,135,000	1,873,000	2,079,204
Cotton	570,000	641,000	603,594
Coffee.	487,000	343,000	429,501
Ground-nuts	210,000	277,000	257,807
Hides .	131,000	161,000	224,907
Copra	38,000	82,000	104,757
Grain .	..	..	126,413
Gold .	370,000	490,000	526,277

* Includes re-exports.

Appendix III

Country	Exports to 1936	Exports to 1937	Imports from 1936	Imports from 1937
	£	£	£	£
U.K.	998,000	1,030,000	914,000	953,000
Kenya and Uganda	807,000	923,000	278,000	363,000
British India	269,000	418,000	169,000	210,000
Other British countries	195,000	209,000	99,000	109,000
Total, British Empire	2,202,000	2,505,000	1,460,000	1,636,000
Germany	326,000	501,000	473,000	526,000
U.S.A.	310,000	232,000	217,000	254,000
Belgium	574,000	596,000	—	—
Japan	—	—	781,000	934,000
France	170,000	202,000	—	—
Total, foreign countries	1,824,000	1,938,000	1,897,000	2,288,000

2. British Cameroons.

	1936	1937
	£	£
Total imports	243,467	328,943
Total exports	445,459	526,554
Chief exports:		
Dried bananas	11,492	15,473
Palm kernels	12,221	17,397
Palm oil	24,132	30,372
Cocoa	114,000	132,000
Rubber	20,585	36,353

Country	Exports to (1937)	Imports from (1937)
	(Per cent.)	(Per cent.)
U.K.	6·4	11·9
Germany	79·75	47·57
Holland	7·22	1·5
British Empire	—	7·5
U.S.A.	—	1·7
Japan	—	16
Norway	—	3·8
French Cameroons	5·78	—

3. South West Africa.

	1935	1936	1937
	£	£	£
Total imports	1,486,000	1,941,000	2,459,000
Total exports	2,512,946	3,106,916	3,690,686
Chief exports:			
Diamonds	115,000	896,000	916,918
Vanadium	57,000	213,151	202,000
Copper ore	57,000	—	189,000
Tin ore	10,000	40,000	38,000
Hides and skins	24,000	19,000	16,826
Karakul pelts	190,000	754,000	1,222,629
Cattle for slaughter	148,000	306,000	171,000
Sheep and goats for slaughter	137,000	48,000	72,000
Preserved fish	146,000	91,000	85,000
Wool	40,000	123,000	148,000
Butter	228,000	337,000	344,000

Country	Imports (1937)	Exports (1937)
	(Per cent.)	(Per cent.)
Union of S. Africa	39.5	16.4
British Empire (except S. Africa)	5.9	53.7
Foreign countries	27.5	—
Re-exports through S. Africa	27.5	—
Germany[1]	—	15.5
Other foreign countries	—	12

[1] In this case separate figures for Germany are only obtainable for exports: under imports Germany is included in Foreign countries.

4. British Togoland.

	1936	1937
	£	£
Imports	10,123	16,208
Exports	191,523	111,859

[In British Togoland there are customs posts only on the eastern, not on the western boundary. All imports and exports, wherever ultimately brought from, or sent to, are labelled for French Togoland. Figures in this case from Official Report for the Territory, 1938.]

Appendix III

5. New Guinea.

	1935–6	1936–7
	£	£
Total imports	1,139,000	1,113,000
Total exports	2,059,000	2,712,000
Chief exports:		
Copra	609,000	985,000
Coco-nut	52,704	69,544
Gold	1,364,000	1,617,000

	Imports from		Exports to	
Country	1935–6	1936–7	1935–6	1936–7
	£	£	£	£
U.K.	148,000	119,000	211,000	231,000
Australia	434,000	431,000	197,000	246,000
Rest of British Empire	49,000	67,000	—	5,000
Germany[1]	44,000	51,000	—	—
European countries	—	—	273,000	492,000
U.S.A.	164,000	172,000	—	32,000
Other foreign countries	194,000	209,000	14,000	89,000

6. West Samoa.

	1936	1937
	£	£
Total imports	129,000	214,000
Total exports*	211,000	282,000
Chief exports:		
Copra	125,000	160,000
Cocoa	37,286	56,910
Bananas	37,390	56,358

* Includes re-exports.

[1] In this case separate figures for Germany are only obtainable for imports: under exports Germany is included in European countries.

	Imports from		Exports to	
Country	1936	1937	1936	1937
	£	£	£	£
U.K.	25,000	34,000	52,000	53,000
Australia	22,000	33,000	—	—
New Zealand	38,000	57,000	40,000	59,000
Rest of British Empire	13,000	28,000	1,000	9,000
U.S.A.	9,000	17,000	11,000	44,000
Other foreign countries	22,000	45,000	99,000	114,000

7. Nauru.

	1936	1937
	£	£
Total imports	120,000	116,000
Total exports	376,000	411,000
Chief export:		
Phosphates	376,000	411,000

Country	Imports from (1937)	Exports to (1937)
	£	£
Australia	73,000	276,000
U.K.	12,000	4,723
New Zealand	—	117,000
Other British countries	4,000	4,000
Germany	11,000	—
U.S.A.	9,000	—
Japan	—	11,000
Other foreign countries	7,000	3,000

APPENDIX IV

POPULATION OF THE GERMAN COLONIES IN 1913 AND OF THE MANDATED TERRITORIES TO-DAY

Country	Year	Natives	Whites	Asiatics†	Area in sq. miles
1. German East Africa	1913–14	7,645,770	5,336	...	393,500
Tanganyika	1935	5,096,178	8,455	33,447	360,000
Ruanda-Urundi	1935	3,385,707	893	580	15,000
2. German South West Africa	1913–14	80,556	14,830	—	322,000
South West Africa	1936	328,467	31,049	—	317,725
3. Kamerun	1913–14	3,326,132(4)	1,871	...	197,498(4)
British Cameroons	1935	817,616	354	—	34,081
French Cameroons	1935	2,338,781	2,257	67	143,415
4. Togo	1913–14	1,031,978	368	...	34,600
British Togoland	1931	293,671	43	—	13,041
French Togoland	1935	762,947	418	55	20,464
5. Kaiser Wilhelmsland (3)	1913–14	719,000	968	...	90,000
New Guinea Mandated Territory (3)	1935	484,734	2,971	1,603	93,300
6. Western Samoa	1913–14	35,000	557	...	..
,, ,,	1936	55,057	367	522	..
7. Nauru	1936	1,647	179	1,092	8

KEY: ... figures not known or unobtainable. — no population of this class.

† When there are no separate figures given, the Asiatic population is included under Whites.

NOTES: (1) The figures for the German colonies in 1913–14 are taken from Dr. Townsend, *The Rise and Fall of the German Colonial Empire*, pp. 265–6. Those for the present Mandated Territories are taken from

[continued overleaf]

R. R. Kuczynski, *Colonial Population* (Oxford, 1938), pp. 17–21. For New Guinea the figures are taken from *The Colonial Problem* (R.I.I.A., Oxford, 1937), p. 352.

(2) The figures given for the German colonies in 1913–14 do not distinguish between Whites and Asiatics.

(3) Kaiser Wilhelmsland and the New Guinea Mandated Territory include not only the territory on the mainland of New Guinea, but also the Bismarck Archipelago. The figure for the New Guinea Mandated Territory in 1935 is for the enumerated native population.

(4) The figures given by H. R. Rudin (op. cit., p. 102) are: Native population, 2,650,000; Area, 292,000 sq. miles.

The figures for 1913–14 and for the present day are not always on the same basis and this may account for certain rather striking differences, e.g. in S.W. Africa, where, although the official German figures give a native population of 80,556, the actual number of natives living within the whole of the territory was far higher.

APPENDIX V

THE CONGO BASIN TREATY

THE international obligations in regard to the Congo Basin are embodied in three treaties:

General Act of the Berlin Conference, signed February 26, 1885.

General Act of the Brussels Conference, signed July 2, 1890.

Convention of St. Germain-en-Laye, signed September 10, 1919.

The two latter treaties are in the nature of revisions of the Berlin Act.

The principal provisions of the Berlin Act are as follows:

(1) 'The trade of all nations shall enjoy complete freedom in all the regions forming the basin of the Congo and its outlets . . . .'[1]

(2) 'All flags, without distinction of nationality, shall have free access to the whole of the coastline of the territories above enumerated: to the rivers there running into the sea, to all waters of the Congo and its affluents, including the lakes, and to all the ports situate on the banks of these waters . . .'

(3) 'Wares, of whatever origin, imported into these regions, under whatsoever flag, by sea or river or overland, shall be subject to no other taxes than such as may be levied as fair compensation for expenditure in the interests of trade, and which for this reason must be

[1] The Congo Basin includes the Belgian Congo, Uganda, Kenya, Tanganyika, Ruanda-Urundi, Nyasaland; and parts of Angola, Mozambique, French Equatorial Africa, Italian Somaliland, Northern Rhodesia, and the Cameroons.

equally borne by the subjects themselves and by foreigners of all nationalities. All differential dues on vessels as well as merchandize, are forbidden.'

(4) 'Merchandize imported into these regions shall remain free from import and transit dues.'

(5) 'No Power which exercises or shall exercise sovereign rights in the above-mentioned regions shall be allowed to grant therein a monopoly or favour of any kind in matters of trade.'

(6) 'All the Powers exercising sovereign rights or influence in the aforesaid territories bind themselves to watch over the preservation of the native tribes, and to care for the improvement of the conditions of their moral and material well-being, and to help in suppressing slavery, and especially the slave-trade.

'They shall, without distinction of creed or nation, protect and favour all religious, scientific, or charitable institutions and undertakings created and organized for the above ends, or which aim at instructing the natives and bringing home to them the blessings of civilization.

'Christian missionaries, scientists, and explorers, with their followers, property, and collections, shall likewise be the objects of especial protection.

'Freedom of conscience and religious toleration are expressly guaranteed to the natives, no less than to subjects and foreigners.

'The free and public exercise of all forms of Divine worship, and the right to build edifices for religious purposes, and to organize religious missions belonging to all creeds, shall not be limited or fettered in any way whatsoever.'

(9) . . . 'the Powers which do or shall exercise sovereign rights or influence in the territories forming the conventional basin of the Congo declare that these terri-

tories may not serve as a market, or means of transit, for the trade in slaves, of whatever race they may be.'

(10) . . . 'the High Signatory Powers to the present Act and those who shall hereafter adopt it, bind themselves to respect the neutrality of the territories belonging to the said countries, comprising therein the territorial waters, so long as the Powers which exercise or shall exercise sovereignty or Protectorate over those territories, using their option of proclaiming themselves neutral, shall fulfil the duties which neutrality requires.'

(11) 'In case a Power exercising rights of sovereignty or Protectorate in the countries mentioned in Article I, and placed under the free trade system, shall be involved in a war, then the High Signatory Powers to the present Act, and those who shall hereafter adopt it, bind themselves to lend their good offices in order that the territories belonging to this Power and comprised in the Conventional free trade zone shall, by the common consent of this Power and the other belligerents, be placed during the War under the rule of neutrality . . .'

(12) 'In case a serious disagreement originating on the subject of, or in the limits of, the territories mentioned in Article I, and placed under the free trade system, shall arise between any Signatory Powers of the present Act, or the Powers which may become parties to it, these Powers bind themselves, before appealing to arms, to have recourse to the mediation of one or more friendly Powers.'

(13) 'The navigation of the Congo, without excepting any of its branches or outlets, is, and shall remain, free for the merchant ships of all nations equally, whether carrying cargo or ballast, for the transport of goods or passengers . . .'

Then follow various articles providing for the free

navigation of the Congo River, and similar provisions for the free navigation of the Niger River.

(34) 'Any Power which henceforth takes possession of a tract of land on the coasts of the African Continent outside of the present possessions, or which, hitherto without such possessions, shall acquire them, as well as the Power which assumes a Protectorate there, shall accompany the respective act with a notification thereof, addressed to the other Signatory Powers of the present Act, in order to enable them, if need be, to make good any claims of their own.'

(35) 'The Signatory Powers of the present Act recognize the obligation to insure the establishment of authority in regions occupied by them on the coasts of the African Continent sufficient to protect existing rights, and, as the case may be, freedom of trade and of transit under the conditions agreed upon.'

The Berlin Act was signed by Great Britain, Germany, Austro-Hungary, Belgium, Denmark, Spain, the United States, France, Italy, Holland, Portugal, Russia, Sweden and Norway, and Turkey.

The Brussels Act dealt in much greater detail with provisions for the suppression of the slave-trade, the importation of arms and ammunition, and the liquor traffic. By it an international office was set up at Zanzibar for centralizing all information about the slave trade and facilitating its suppression. Its provisions were adopted by the former states, together with the Sultanate of Zanzibar, and Persia.

The Convention of St. Germain-en-Laye contained the following provisions:

(1) In so far as related to their own territories the Signatory Powers guaranteed freedom of trade to all nations, within the conventional Basin of the Congo.

Appendix V

(2) Free access to the interior was guaranteed to nationals of all Signatory Powers. No differential treatment was to be given, and no duties or taxes imposed other than for services rendered. Subject to these provisions the States reserved complete liberty of action as to tariffs, customs, and navigation regulations.

(3) The rights and protection of nationals of the Signatory Powers were guaranteed within the Territories enumerated.

(4) 'Each state reserves the right to dispose freely of its property and to grant concessions for the development of the natural resources of the territory, but no regulations on these matters shall admit of differential treatment between the nationals of the Signatory Powers . . .'

(5–9) Revised provisions for the free and equal navigation of the Niger and its tributaries.

(10) 'The Signatory Powers recognize the obligation to maintain in the territories subject to their jurisdiction an authority and police force sufficient to ensure protection of persons and property, and, if necessary, freedom of trade and of transit.'

(11) Reaffirms the main provisions of Article 6 of the Berlin Act.

(12) Disputes to be submitted to arbitration in conformity with the provisions of the League Covenant.

This Covention was signed by the United States, Belgium, the British Empire, France, Italy, Japan, and Portugal. The same powers signed at the same time a Convention relating to the Liquor Traffic in Africa.

The provisions of the Berlin and Brussels Acts for the suppression of slavery and the slave-trade were reaffirmed and reinforced by the League of Nations Slavery Convention, signed at Geneva, September 25, 1926.

APPENDIX VI[1]

REPLY OF THE ALLIED AND ASSOCIATED POWERS TO THE OBSERVATIONS OF THE GERMAN DELEGATION ON THE CONDITIONS OF PEACE
16 JUNE 1919

Covering Letter to the President of the German Delegation, June 16, 1919.

Sir,

The Allied and Associated Powers have given the most earnest consideration to the observations of the German Delegation on the Conditions of Peace. The reply protests against the peace both on the grounds that it conflicts with the terms upon which the Armistice of November 11, 1918, was signed, and that it is a peace of violence and not of justice. The protest of the German Delegation shows that they utterly fail to understand the position in which Germany stands to-day. They seem to think that Germany has only to 'make sacrifices in order to attain peace', as if this were but the end of some mere struggle for territory and power.

The Allied and Associated Powers therefore feel it necessary to begin their reply by a clear statement of the judgement passed upon the war by practically the whole of civilised mankind.

I

In the view of the Allied and Associated Powers the war which began on August 1, 1914, was the greatest crime against humanity and the freedom of peoples that any nation, calling itself civilised, has ever consciously

[1] The complete text is to be found in *British and Foreign State Papers*, 1919, vol. cxii (H.M.S.O., 1922), pp. 244–316.

Appendix VI

committed. For many years the rulers of Germany, true to the Prussian tradition, strove for a position of dominance in Europe. They were not satisfied with that growing prosperity and influence to which Germany was entitled, and which all other nations were willing to accord her, in the society of free and equal peoples. They required that they should be able to dictate to and tyrannise over a subservient Europe, as they dictated to and tyrannised over a subservient Germany.

In order to attain their ends they used every channel in their power through which to educate their subjects in the doctrine that might was right in international affairs. They never ceased to expand German armaments by land and sea, and to propagate the falsehood that this was necessary because Germany's neighbours were jealous of her prosperity and power. They sought to sow hostility and suspicion instead of friendship between nations. They developed a system of espionage and intrigue which enabled them to stir up internal rebellion and unrest and even to make secret offensive preparations within the territory of their neighbours whereby they might, when the moment came, strike them down with greater certainty and ease. They kept Europe in a ferment by threats of violence, and when they found that their neighbours were resolved to resist their arrogant will, they determined to assert their predominance in Europe by force. As soon as their preparations were complete, they encouraged a subservient ally to declare war against Serbia at forty-eight hours' notice, knowing full well that a conflict involving the control of the Balkans could not be localised and almost certainly meant a general war. In order to make doubly sure, they refused every attempt at conciliation and conference until it was too late, and the world war was inevitable for which they had plotted, and for which alone among the nations they were fully equipped and prepared.

Germany's responsibility, however, is not confined to having planned and started the war. She is no less responsible for the savage and inhuman manner in which it was conducted.

Though Germany was herself a guarantor of Belgium, the rulers of Germany violated, after a solemn promise to respect it, the neutrality of this unoffending people. Not content with this they deliberately carried out a series of promiscuous shootings and burnings with the sole object of terrifying the inhabitants into submission by the very frightfulness of their action. They were the first to use poisonous gas, notwithstanding the appalling suffering it entailed. They began the bombing and long-distance shelling of towns for no military object, but solely for the purpose of reducing the morale of their opponents by striking at their women and children. They commenced the submarine campaign with its piratical challenge to international law, and its destruction of great numbers of innocent passengers and sailors, in mid-ocean, far from succour, at the mercy of the winds and waves, and the yet more ruthless submarine crews. They drove thousands of men and women and children with brutal savagery into slavery in foreign lands. They allowed barbarities to be practised against their prisoners of war from which the most uncivilised peoples would have recoiled. The conduct of Germany is almost unexampled in human history. The terrible responsibility which lies at her doors can be seen in the fact that not less than 7,000,000 dead lie buried in Europe, while more than 20,000,000 others carry upon them the evidence of wounds and sufferings, because Germany saw fit to gratify her lust for tyranny by resort to war.

Appendix VI

The Allied and Associated Powers believe that they will be false to those who have given their all to save the freedom of the world, if they consent to treat this war on any other basis than as a crime against humanity and right.

This attitude of the Allied and Associated Powers was made perfectly clear to Germany during the war by their principal statesmen. It was defined by President Wilson in his speech of April 6, 1918, and explicitly and categorically accepted by the German people as a principle governing the peace:

'Let everything that we say, my fellow countrymen, everything that we henceforth plan and accomplish, ring true to this response till the majesty and might of our concerted power shall fill the thought and utterly defeat the force of those who flout and misprise what we honour and hold dear. Germany has once said that force, and force alone, shall decide whether justice and peace shall reign in the affairs of men, whether Right as America conceives it, or Dominion as she conceives it, shall determine the destinies of mankind. There is, therefore, but one response possible from us: Force, Force to the utmost, Force without stint or limit, righteous and triumphant Force which shall make Right the law of the world, and cast every selfish dominion down in the dust.'

It was set forth clearly in a speech of the Prime Minister of Great Britain, of December 14, 1917:

'There is no security in any land without certainty of punishment. There is no protection for life, property or money in a State when the criminal is more powerful than the law. The law of nations is no exception, and, until it has been vindicated, the peace of the world will always be at the mercy of any nation whose professors have assiduously taught it to believe that no crime is wrong so long as it leads to the aggrandisement and enrichment of the country to which they owe allegiance. There have been many times in the history of the world criminal States. We are dealing with one of them now. And there will always be criminal States until the reward of international crime becomes too precarious to make it profitable, and the punishment of international crime becomes too sure to make it attractive.'

It was made clear also in an address of M. Clemenceau, of September 1918:

'What do they [the French soldiers] want? What do we ourselves want? To fight, to fight victoriously and unceasingly, until the hour when the enemy shall understand that no compromise is possible between such crime and "justice". . . . We only seek peace, and we wish to make it just and permanent, in order that future generations may be saved from the abominations of the past.'

Similarly, Signor Orlando, speaking on October 3, 1918, declared:

'We shall obtain Peace when our enemies recognise that humanity has the right and duty to safeguard itself against a continuation of such causes as have brought about this terrible slaughter; and that the blood of millions of men calls not for vengeance but for the realisation of those high ideals for which it has been so generously shed. Nobody thinks of employing—even by way of legitimate retaliation—methods of brutal violence or of overbearing domination or of suffocation of the freedom of any people—methods and

Appendix VI

policies which made the whole world rise against the Central Powers. But nobody will contend that the moral order can be restored simply because he who fails in his iniquitous endeavour declares that he has renounced his aim. Questions intimately affecting the peace of Nations, once raised, must obtain the solution which Justice requires.'

Justice, therefore, is the only possible basis for the settlement of the accounts of this terrible war. Justice is what the German Delegation asks for and says that Germany had been promised. Justice is what Germany shall have. But it must be justice for all. There must be justice for the dead and wounded and for those who have been orphaned and bereaved that Europe might be freed from Prussian despotism. There must be justice for the peoples who now stagger under war debts which exceed £30,000,000,000 that liberty might be saved. There must be justice for those millions whose homes and land, ships and property, German savagery has spoliated and destroyed.

That is why the Allied and Associated Powers have insisted as a cardinal feature of the Treaty that Germany must undertake to make reparation to the very uttermost of her power; for reparation for wrongs inflicted is of the essence of justice. That is why they insist that those individuals who are most clearly responsible for German aggression and for those acts of barbarism and inhumanity which have disgraced the German conduct of the war, must be handed over to a justice which has not been meted out to them at home. That, too, is why Germany must submit for a few years to certain special disabilities and arrangements. Germany has ruined the industries, the mines, and the machinery of neighbouring countries, not during battle, but with the deliberate and calculated purpose of enabling her industries to seize their markets before their industries could recover from the devastation thus wantonly inflicted upon them. Germany has despoiled her neighbours of everything she could make use of or carry away. Germany has destroyed the shipping of all nations on the high seas, when there was no chance of rescue for their passengers and crews. It is only justice that restitution should be made and that these wronged peoples should be safeguarded for a time from the competition of a nation whose industries are intact and have even been fortified by machinery stolen from occupied territories. If these things are hardships for Germany, they are hardships which Germany has brought upon herself. Somebody must suffer for the consequences of the war. Is it to be Germany, or only the peoples she has wronged?

Not to do justice to all concerned would only leave the world open to fresh calamities. If the German people themselves, or any other nation, are to be deterred from following the footsteps of Prussia, if mankind is to be lifted out of the belief that war for selfish ends is legitimate to any State, if the old era is to be left behind and nations as well as individuals are to be brought beneath the reign of law, even if there is to be early reconciliation and appeasement, it will be because those responsible for concluding the war have had the courage to see that justice is not deflected for the sake of convenient peace.

It is said that the German Revolution ought to make a difference, and that the German people are not responsible for the policy of the rulers whom they have thrown from power. The Allied and Associated Powers recognise and welcome the change. It represents a great hope for peace, and for a new European order in the future.

Appendix VI

But it cannot affect the settlement of the war itself. The German Revolution was stayed until the German armies had been defeated in the field, and all hope of profiting by a war of conquest had vanished. Throughout the war, as before the war, the German people and their representatives supported the war, voted the credits, subscribed to the war loans, obeyed every order, however savage, of their Government. They shared the responsibility for the policy of their Government, for at any moment, had they willed it, they could have reversed it. Had that policy succeeded they would have acclaimed it with the same enthusiasm with which they welcomed the outbreak of the war. They cannot now pretend, having changed their rulers after the war was lost, that it is justice that they should escape the consequences of their deeds.

II

The Allied and Associated Powers therefore believe that the peace they have proposed is fundamentally a peace of justice. They are no less certain that it is a peace of right fulfilling the terms agreed upon at the time of the armistice. There can be no doubt as to the intentions of the Allied and Associated Powers to base the settlement of Europe on the principle of freeing oppressed peoples, and re-drawing national boundaries as far as possible in accordance with the will of the peoples concerned, while giving to each facilities for living an independent national and economic life. These intentions were made clear, not only in President Wilson's address to Congress of January 8, 1918, but in 'the principles of settlement enunciated in his subsequent addresses', which were the agreed basis of the peace. . . .

Clemenceau's letter then proceeds to expound the settlement on each of the disputed points: Poland, Danzig, the Saar, Denmark's and Belgium's recovery of territory.

Finally, the Allied and Associated Powers are satisfied that the native inhabitants of the German colonies are strongly opposed to being brought again under Germany's sway, and the record of German rule, the traditions of the German Government, and the use to which these colonies were put as bases from which to prey upon the commerce of the world, make it impossible for the Allied and Associated Powers to return them to Germany, or to entrust to her the responsibility for the training and education of their inhabitants. . . .

III

Clemenceau here deals with the proposals in regard to international control of rivers.

IV and V

Clemenceau deals with the economic and financial conditions.

VI

Clemenceau explains reasons for the refusal to admit Germany to the League of Nations.

VII

Clemenceau gives reasons for the blockade of Germany.

VIII

In conclusion the Allied and Associated Powers must make it clear that this letter and the memorandum attached constitute their last word.

They have examined the German observations and counter-proposals with earnest attention and care. They have, in consequence, made important practical concessions, but in its principles they stand by the Treaty. They believe that it is not only a just settlement of the

Appendix VI 255

Great War, but that it provides the basis upon which the peoples of Europe can live together in friendship and equality. At the same time it creates the machinery for the peaceful adjustment of all international problems by discussion and consent, whereby the settlement of 1919 itself can be modified from time to time to suit new facts and new conditions as they arise.

It is frankly not based upon a general condonation of the events of 1914-1918. It would not be a peace of justice if it were. But it represents a sincere and deliberate attempt to establish 'that reign of law, based upon the consent of the governed, and sustained by the organized opinion of mankind' which was the agreed basis of the peace.

As such the Treaty in its present form must be accepted or rejected. . . .

The letter concludes with a declaration that, unless the Treaty is accepted within five days, the Armistice will be considered at an end, and the Allies will take the necessary steps to enforce their terms. The letter is signed by Clemenceau.

REPLY OF THE ALLIED AND ASSOCIATED POWERS
INTRODUCTION
Basis of the Peace Negotiations

The Allied and Associated Powers are in complete accord with the German Delegation in their insistence that the basis for the negotiation of the Treaty of Peace is to be found in the correspondence which immediately preceded the signing of the Armistice on November 11, 1918. It was there agreed that the Treaty of Peace should be based upon the Fourteen Points of President Wilson's address of January 8, 1918, as they were modified by the Allies' memorandum included in the President's note of November 5, 1918, and upon the principles of settlement enunciated by President Wilson in his later addresses, and particularly in his address of September 27, 1918. These are the principles upon which hostilities were abandoned in November 1918, these are the principles upon which the Allied and Associated Powers agreed that Peace might be based, these are the principles which have guided them in the deliberations which have led to the formulation of the Conditions of Peace.

It is now contended by the German Delegation that the Conditions of Peace do not conform to these principles which had thus become binding upon the Allied and Associated Powers as well as upon the Germans themselves. In an attempt to prove a breach of this agreement the German Delegation have drawn quotations from a number of speeches, most of which were before the Address to Congress and many of which were uttered by Allied statesmen at a time when they were not at war with Germany, or had no responsibility for the conduct of public affairs. The Allied and Associated Powers consider it unnecessary, therefore, to oppose this list of detached quotations with others equally irrelevant to a discussion concerning the basis of the peace negotiations. In answer to the implication of these quotations, it is sufficient to refer to a note of the Allied Powers transmitted to the President of the United States on January 10, 1917, in response to an enquiry as to the conditions upon which they would be prepared to make peace:

'The Allies feel a desire as deep as that of the United States Government to see ended, at the earliest possible moment, the war for which the Central Empires are responsible, and which inflicts sufferings so cruel upon

Appendix VI

humanity. But they judge it impossible to-day to bring about a peace that shall assure to them the reparation, the restitution, and the guarantees to which they are entitled by the aggression for which the responsibility lies upon the Central Empires—and of which the very principle tended to undermine the safety of Europe—a peace which shall also permit the establishment upon firm foundations of the future of the nations of Europe.'

In the same note, in addition to a reference to Poland, they declared the War Aims of the Allies to include:

'. . . first of all, the restoration of Belgium, Serbia, and Montenegro, with the compensation due to them; the evacuation of the invaded territories in France, in Russia, in Rumania with just reparation; the reorganization of Europe, guaranteed by a stable régime and based at once on respect for nationalities and on the right to full security and liberty of economic development possessed by all peoples, small and great, and at the same time upon territorial conventions and international settlements such as to guarantee land and sea frontiers against unjustified attacks; the restitution of provinces formerly torn away from the Allies by force against the wish of their inhabitants; the liberation of the Italians, as also of the Slavs, Rumanians and Czecho-Slovaks from foreign domination; the setting free of the populations subject to the bloody tyranny of the Turks; and the turning out of Europe of the Ottoman Empire as decidedly foreign to Western civilization.'

It cannot be disputed that responsible statesmen, those qualified to express the will of the peoples of the Allied and Associated Powers, have never entertained or expressed a desire for any other peace than one which should undo the wrongs of 1914, vindicate justice and international right, and reconstruct the political foundations of Europe on lines which would give liberty to all its peoples, and therefore the prospect of a lasting peace.

But the German Delegation profess to find discrepancies between the agreed basis of peace and the draft of the Treaty. They discover a contradiction between the terms of the Treaty and a statement taken from an address delivered at Baltimore on April 6, 1918, by President Wilson:

'We are ready, whenever the final reckoning is made, to be just to the German people, as with all others. . . . To propose anything but justice to Germany at any time, whatever the outcome of the war, would be to renounce our own cause, for we ask nothing that we are not willing to accord.'

This quotation does not stand alone. It should be read in conjunction with one of the cardinal principles of the Mount Vernon address of July 4, 1918, which demanded:

'The destruction of every arbitrary power everywhere that can separately, secretly, and of its single choice disturb the peace of the world or, if it cannot be presently destroyed, at the least its reduction to virtual impotence.'

Neither of these two principles of the agreed basis of peace has been lost sight of in the formulation of these Conditions.

The German Delegation see in the provisions with regard to territorial settlements a conflict between the terms of the Treaty and the following statement made by President Wilson on June 9, 1918:

'If it is indeed and in truth the mutual aim of the Governments allied against Germany and of their nations, in the coming negotiations of peace to bring

Appendix VI

about a sure and lasting peace, all who sit down at the table of negotiations will be ready and willing to pay the only price for which it can be gotten. . . . This price is impartial justice in every item without regard to whose interests may be crossed by it, and not only impartial justice but also satisfaction to all nations whose future is to be decided upon.'

In their communication they enumerate a number of territorial settlements and conclude that 'their basis is indifferently, now the consideration of an unchangeable historical right, now the principle of ethnographical facts, now the consideration of economical interests. In every case the decision is against Germany'.

If in certain cases, not in all, the decision has in fact not been in favour of Germany, this is not the result of any purpose to act unjustly towards Germany. It is the inevitable result of the fact that an appreciable portion of the territory of the German Empire consisted of districts which had in the past been wrongfully appropriated by Prussia or by Germany. It is the chief duty of the Allied and Associated Powers to rectify these injustices in accordance with the explicit statement of President Wilson in his address to Congress on February 11, 1918:

'Each part of the final settlement must be based upon the essential justice of that particular case and upon such adjustments as are most likely to bring a peace that will be permanent.'

The German Delegation find a conflict between the terms of the Treaty which set forth the economic provisions and the third of President Wilson's Fourteen Points:

'The removal, so far as possible, of all economic barriers and the establishment of an equality of trade conditions among all the nations consenting to the peace and associating themselves for its maintenance.'

In their application of this principle the German Delegation would neglect entirely the economic conditions which have resulted from the war, with their own country intact and in no wise suffering from the devastation brought upon the lands and homes of the Allied peoples. They nevertheless seek immediate admission to all of the trade arrangements which are to be provided for by the Conditions of Peace. This would have the effect of establishing an inequality of trade conditions which would continue in Europe for many years to come. Equality can only be established by arrangements which take into account the existing differences in economic strength and industrial integrity of the peoples of Europe. But the Conditions of Peace contain some provisions for the future which may outlast the transition period during which the economic balance is to be restored; and a reciprocity is foreseen after that period which is very clearly that equality of trade conditions for which President Wilson has stipulated.

The German Delegation profess to find in the terms of the Treaty a violation of the principle expressed by President Wilson before Congress on February 11, 1918:

'That peoples and provinces are not to be bartered about from sovereignty to sovereignty as if they were mere chattels and pawns in a game.'

The Allied and Associated Powers emphatically reject the suggestion that there has been any 'bartering about' of peoples and provinces. Every territorial settlement of the Treaty of Peace has been determined upon after most careful and laboured consideration of all the religious, racial, and linguistic factors in each particular country.

Appendix VI

The legitimate hopes of peoples long under alien rule have been heard; and the decisions in each instance have been founded upon the principle explicitly enunciated in the same address; that

> 'All well-defined national aspirations shall be accorded the utmost satisfaction that can be accorded them without introducing new or perpetuating old elements of discord and antagonism that would be likely in time to break the peace of Europe and consequently of the world.'

Finally, the German Delegation take exception to the fact that Germany has not been invited to join in the formation of the League of Nations as an original member. President Wilson's declarations, however, envisaged no league of nations which would include Germany at the outset, and no statement of his can be adduced in support of this contention. Indeed, in his speech of September 27, 1918, he laid down with the greatest precision the conditions which must govern her admission:

> 'It is necessary to guarantee the peace, and the peace cannot be guaranteed as an afterthought. The reason, to speak in plain terms again, why it must be guaranteed, is that there will be parties to the peace whose promises have proved untrustworthy, and means must be found in connection with the peace settlement itself to remove that source of insecurity.'

and further,

> 'Germany will have to redeem her character not by what happens at the peace table, but by what follows.'

The Allied and Associated Powers look forward to the time when the League of Nations established by this Treaty shall extend its membership to all peoples; but they cannot abandon any of the essential conditions of an enduring League.

. . . . . .

Then follows the detailed reply of the Allied and Associated Powers, subdivided into fourteen sections, as follows:

I. *The League of Nations.*

II and III. *Boundaries of Germany and political clauses in Europe.*

IV. *German rights and interests outside Germany.*

V. *Military, naval, and air clauses.*

VI. *Prisoners of war.*

VII. *Responsibilities of Germany in the War.*

VIII. *Reparation.*

IX. *Financial Clauses.*

X. *Economic Clauses.*

XII. *Ports, waterways, and railways.*

XIII. *Labour.*

XIV. *Guarantees.*

We print below the whole of Part IV, the section which deals with the Colonial settlement.

Part IV

German rights and interests outside Germany

I

In requiring Germany to renounce all her rights and claims to her overseas possessions, the Allied and Associated Powers placed before every other consideration the interests of the native populations advocated by President Wilson in the fifth point of his Fourteen Points mentioned in his address of January 8, 1918. Reference to the evidence from German sources previous to the war of an official as well as of a private character, and to the formal charges made in the Reichstag,

Appendix VI

especially by MM. Erzberger and Noske, will suffice to throw full light upon the German colonial administration, upon the cruel methods of repression, the arbitrary requisition, and the various forms of forced labour which resulted in the depopulation of vast expanses of territory in German East Africa, and the Cameroons, not to mention the tragic fate of the Hereros in South West Africa, which is well known to all.

Germany's dereliction in the sphere of colonial civilization has been revealed too completely to admit of the Allied and Associated Powers consenting to make a second experiment and of their assuming the responsibility of again abandoning thirteen or fourteen millions of natives to a fate from which the war has delivered them.

Moreover, the Allied and Associated Powers felt themselves compelled to safeguard their own security and the Peace of the world against a military imperialism, which sought to establish bases whence it could pursue a policy of interference and intimidation against the other Powers.

II

The Allied and Associated Powers considered that the loss of her Colonies would not hinder Germany's normal economic development.

The trade of the German Colonies has never represented more than a very small fraction of Germany's total trade: in 1913 one-half of one per cent. of her imports and one-half of one per cent. of her exports. Of the total volume imported by Germany of such products as cotton, cocoa, rubber, palm-kernels, tobacco, jute, and copra, only 3 per cent. came from her Colonies. It is obvious that the financial, commercial, and industrial rehabilitation of Germany must depend on other factors.

For climatic reasons and other natural causes the

German Colonies are incapable of accommodating more than a very small proportion of the excess German emigration. The small number of colonists resident there before the war is conclusive evidence in this respect.

III

The Allied and Associated Powers have drawn up, in the matter of the cession of the German Colonies, the following methods of procedure, which are in conformity with the rules of International Law and Equity:

(a) The Allied and Associated Powers are applying to the German Colonies the general principle in accordance with which the transfer of sovereignty involves the transfer under the same conditions to the State to which the surrender is made of the immovable and movable property of the ceding State.

They see no reason for consenting in the case of the Colonies to any departure from that principle which may have been admitted as an exceptional measure in the case of territory in Europe.

(b) They are of opinion that the Colonies should not bear any portion of the German debt, nor remain under any obligation to refund to Germany the expenses incurred by the Imperial administration of the Protectorate. In fact, they consider that it would be unjust to burden the natives with expenditure which appears to have been incurred in Germany's own interest, and that it would be no less unjust to make this responsibility rest upon the Mandatory Powers which, in so far as they may be appointed Trustees by the League of Nations, will derive no benefit from such Trusteeship.

IV

The Allied and Associated Powers considered that it would be necessary in the interest of the natives, as well

Appendix VI

as in that of general peace, to restrict the influence which Germany might seek to exert over her former colonies and over the territories of the Allied and Associated Powers.

(*a*) They are obliged for the reasons of security already mentioned to reserve to themselves full liberty of action in determining the conditions on which Germans will be allowed to establish themselves in the territories of the former German colonies. Moreover, the control to be exercised by the League of Nations will provide all the necessary guarantees.

(*b*) They require Germany to subscribe to the Conventions which they may conclude for the control of the traffic in Arms and Spirits and for the modification of the General Acts of Berlin and Brussels. They do not think that Germany has any ground to consider herself humiliated or injured because she is required to give her consent in advance to measures accepted by all the great commercial Powers in regard to questions of such great importance to the welfare of the native populations and to the maintenance of civilization and peace.

V

The Allied and Associated Powers consider that all the possessions and property of the German State in the territory of Kiaochow must be treated on the same footing as State property in all the other German overseas possessions, and be transferred without compensation. In this connection they recall the fact that Kiaochow, which was unjustly torn from China, has been used by Germany as a military base in pursuance of a policy which in its various manifestations has constituted a perpetual menace to the peace of the Far East. In these circumstances they see no reason why Germany should be compensated for the loss of works and establishments and in general for public property which in the hand of this Power have for the most part been used merely as a means of carrying out its policy of aggression.

In so far as concerns the railway and the mines that go with it, referred to in Article 156, paragraph 2, the Allied and Associated Powers hold that these should be considered as public property. They would, however, be prepared, in the event of Germany adducing proof to the contrary, to apply to such private rights as German nationals may be able to establish in the matter, the general principles laid down in the Conditions of Peace in respect of compensation of this character.

VI

The Allied and Associated Powers are anxious that no misunderstanding should exist with regard to the disposition of the property of German missions in territory belonging to them or of which the government is entrusted to them in accordance with the Treaty. They have, therefore, explicitly stated that the property of these missions will be handed over to boards of trustees appointed by or approved by the Governments and composed of persons holding the faith of the mission whose property is involved.

TABLE I

[From *Raw Materials and Colonies*, R.I.I.A., p. 29]

	Great Britain and British Colonial Empire*	British Empire as a whole	U.S.A. and Dependencies†	U.S.S.R.	France and Colonies	Germany§	Italy and Colonies	Japanese Empire	Belgium and Colonies	Czechoslovakia‖	Poland
Iron	− −	‡	‡	‡	+	− −	− −	‡	‡	− −	− −
Copper	− −	‡ ‡	‡ ‡ ‡	− −	− −	− −	‡ ‡ ‡	− −	−	− −	+
Lead	− −	‡	‡ ‡ ‡	−	− −	− −	−	−	− −	− −	+
Zinc	− −	‡	− −	− −	− −	− −	− −	‡	− −	− −	−
Tin	+	‡	− −	− −	− −	− −	− −	− −	− −	− −	− −
Bauxite	‡	‡	−	− −	+	− −	‡	− −	− −	− −	− −
Manganese	+	+	− −	+	− −	− −	− −	− −	− −	− −	− −
Nickel	− −	+	− −	− −	‡	− −	− −	−	− −	− −	− −
Tungsten	− −	‡	− −	− −	− −	− −	− −	−	− −	− −	− −
Chromium	− −	‡	− −	−	‡	− −	− −	− −	− −	− −	− −
Vanadium	‡	+	− −	− −	‡	− −	− −	− −	− −	− −	− −
Molybdenum	− −	− −	+	− −	‡	− −	− −	− −	− −	+	− −
Antimony	− −	− −	−	−	− −	−	− −	− −	− −	+	− −
Magnesite	− −	‡	−	‡	− −	−	+	− −	− −	‡	− −
Mercury	− −	− −	− −	‡	− −	− −	+	− −	− −	+	+
Coal	+	+	+	+	− −	+	− −	‡	−	+	‡
Petroleum	− −	− −	+	+	+	− −	− −	− −	− −	− −	− −
Asbestos	− −	+	−	−	+	−	−	‡	− −	+	− −
Graphite	+	+	− −	− −	−	−	−	+	− −	+	− −
Sulphur or Pyrites	−	−	+	− −	− −	− −	+	+	− −	− −	−
Phosphates	‡	‡	+	‡	‡	− −	− −	− −	− −	− −	+
Potash	− −	− −	−	−	+	+	− −	− −	− −	− −	+
Platinum	− −	+	− −	+	− −	− −	− −	− −	− −	− −	− −
Rubber	+	+	− −	− −	‡	− −	− −	− −	−	− −	− −
Cotton	− −	−	+	−	− −	− −	− −	− −	−	− −	−
Wool	−	+	−	− −	− −	− −	− −	− −	− −	− −	− −
Silk	− −	− −	− −	‡	− −	− −	+	+	− −	− −	− −
Flax	− −	− −	− −	+	‡	− −	− −	− −	− −	−	‡
Jute	− −	+	− −	− −	− −	− −	− −	− −	− −	−	−
Hemp	− −	− −	− −	‡	− −	− −	+	− −	− −	−	−
Manila	− −	− −	− −	− −	− −	− −	− −	− −	− −	− −	− −
Sisal	‡	+	− −	− −	− −	− −	− −	− −	− −	− −	− −
Vegetable Oils	‡	+	+	‡	‡	− −	‡	− −	‡	− −	− −
Timber	− −	‡	‡	+	+	− −	− −	−	−	+	+

KEY. + = exportable surplus. ‡ = approximately self-sufficient.
  − = partly dependent on outside sources.
  − − = largely or wholly dependent on outside sources.

* Includes all colonies, protectorates, and mandates, but not the Dominions, India, or S. Rhodesia.
† Excludes the Philippine Islands. ‖ Before 1939.
§ This table was originally compiled at the end of 1935. Recent events—the

[*continued overleaf*]

TABLE IV

TRADE OF METROPOLITAN COUNTRIES WITH THEIR COLONIES

	Imports (as percentage of total imports)				Exports (as percentage of total exports)			
	1934	1935	1936	1937	1934	1935	1936	1937
France	..	25·7	28·5	24·3	..	31·6	33·3	28·3
Belgium*	..	..	7·0	..	..	..	1·1	..
Holland	..	..	7·78	8·14	..	..	5·85	8·16
Portugal	..	..	10·2	11·2	..	..	10·3	12·9
Italy	..	1·6	2·6	2·5	..	14·3	31	25
U.S.A.†	..	..	14·8	..	..	..	12·1	..
Great Britain:								
Colonies	7·4	..	7·6	8·5	9·7	..	10·7	11·1
Dominions‡	29·6	..	31·7	30·9	34·1	..	34·7	33·1
Total all Brit. countries	37	..	39·3	39·4	43·8	..	45·4	44·2
Japan:								
Formosa	..	8·8	..	..	..	12·5	..	..
Korea	..	22·6	..	..	..	19·4	..	..
Manchukuo	..	7·7	..	..	..	5·04	..	..
Kwantung Prov.	..	1·03	..		..	12·01	..	..
Germany (1913)	0·5	..	..	..	0·5	..	..	..

NOTES. * Includes Belgian Congo, but not Ruanda-Urundi.

† Includes Philippine Islands.

‡ Includes Eire, Newfoundland, Canada, Union of S. Africa, New Zealand, Australia, India, and Burma.

SOURCES. *Bulletin statistique générale de la France. Annuaire statistique de la Belgique.* Report on Economic and Commercial Conditions in the Netherlands. (Dept. of Overseas Trade). *Annuário Estatístico de Portugal. Annuario Statistico Italiano.* Statistical Abstract of the U.S.A. Statistical Abstract of the British Empire. Year Book of Japan and Manchukuo.

annexation of Austria and Czechoslovakia by Germany—have rendered it out of date in certain parts. Czechoslovakia has now disappeared as an independent state and her economic resources as shown in this Table must now be incorporated with those of Germany. The political events of 1938 and 1939 therefore mean that Germany has increased her export surplus of coal, and has now export surpluses of graphite and magnesite. She has also added to her stocks of iron, antimony, mercury, and timber; whether the additions are such as to provide her with an export surplus in these materials it is not yet possible to say. The probability is that they have not.

TABLE V
TRADE OF COLONIES WITH THEIR METROPOLITAN COUNTRIES

	Imports (as percentage of total imports)				Exports (as percentage of total exports)			
	1934	1935	1936	1937	1934	1935	1936	1937
Netherlands Indies	..	13·2	16·7	20·2	..	25	28·7	19·5
Belgian Congo	..	..	40·1	..	..	..	77·5	..
French Colonial Empire	..	..	40·3	39·2	..	..	69·3	59·9
Japanese:								
Formosa	..	..	83·3	..	..	..	92·5	..
Korea	..	..	84·9	..	..	..	87·3	..
Kwantung Prov.	..	..	80·9	..	..	..	43·02	..
Mandated islands	..	..	86·2	..	..	..	98·8	..
Italian:								
Eritrea	58·02	..	..	..	72·6	..	..	..
Somaliland	55·5	..	87·7	..	70·1	..	73·2	..
Libya	..	80·5	..	83·8	..	70·7	..	88·3
U.S. Outlying Territories:								
Alaska	..	..	99·3	..	..	..	99·2	..
Puerto Rico	..	..	92·6	..	..	..	98·1	..
Hawaii	..	..	92·7	..	..	..	98·7	..
Philippine Is.	..	..	60·8	..	..	..	80·4	..
American Samoa	..	..	..	..	..	..	25·8	..
Virgin Is.	..	..	61·3	..	..	..	91·5	..
Guam	..	..	51·7	..	..	..	52·7	..
British Colonies:*								
Cyprus	..	..	..	29·7	..	..	..	24·6
Gold Coast	..	..	..	49·1	..	..	..	30·7
Nigeria	..	..	..	54·4	..	..	..	43·5
S. Rhodesia	..	..	..	47·3	..	..	..	35·7
N. Rhodesia	..	..	..	36·3	..	..	..	52
Kenya and Uganda	..	..	..	36·8	..	..	..	22·3
British Malaya	..	..	..	15·4	..	..	..	10·9
Ceylon	..	..	..	22·1	..	..	..	46·3
Hong Kong	..	..	..	7·57	..	..	..	4·4
Jamaica	..	..	..	32·7	..	..	..	55·6
Bermuda	..	..	..	32·9	..	..	..	0
Trinidad and Tobago	..	..	..	35·9	..	..	..	50·8
British Colonial Empire as a whole†	..	..	..	24·5	..	..	..	22·9
Germany (1912)	(1912) 62·1	..	..	..	(1912) 68·3	..	..	..

[*for notes—see overleaf*]

TABLE VI

DENSITY OF POPULATION IN CHIEF EUROPEAN COUNTRIES

Country	Population per sq. kilometre
Netherlands	270
Belgium	267·7
Great Britain	201·5
Germany*	144
Italy	139
Czechoslovakia*	108·09
Switzerland	101·5
Poland	88·2
Austria*	80·6
France	76
Rumania	64·4
Yugoslavia	62·1
U.S.S.R.†	8·2

* Before the annexation of Austria and Czechoslovakia by Germany.

† Includes Asiatic Russia.

NOTES. * All British figures exclude bullion and coin, and re-exports.

† Excludes the Dominions (Eire, Newfoundland, Canada, Australia, New Zealand, Union of S. Africa, India, and Burma). Excludes also British North Borneo, Brunei, Sarawak, Solomon Islands, Falkland Islands, and Mandated Territories.

SOURCES. Economic Review of Foreign Countries (U.S.A. Dept. of Commerce). *Annuaire statistique de la Belgique et du Congo Belge. Bulletin statistique générale de la France. Résumé statistique de l'empire du Japon. Annuario Statistico Italiano.* Statistical Abstract of the U.S.A. Statistical Abstract of the British Empire.

INDEX

Allen of Hurtwood, Lord, 108.
Amery, L. S., 41, 96.
Angelino, A. D. A. de Kat, 101.
Angell, Sir Norman, 79.
Arenberg, 92.
Asquith, H. H. (Lord Oxford), 19.

Baldwin, Stanley (Lord Baldwin), 34.
Barnes, Leonard, 69, 98.
Bebel, A., 92.
Bell, Dr. 39.
Bennett, Benjamin, 137.
Beyers, C. F., 13.
Bismarck, Prince Otto von, 1, 4, 88–90, 118, 145, 169.
Bonn, Dr. M. J., 207.
Borden, Sir Robert, 24.
Botha, General, 11.
Brenner, Dr., 134.
Brookes, E. H., 198.
Buell, R. L., 102.
Burke, Edmund, 198.

Cameron, Sir Donald, 101, 102.
Cana, Frank, 148.
Caprivi, Count, 145.
Carr-Saunders, Prof., 80.
Churchill, Winston, 22, 26.
Clemenceau, 20, 21, 201.
Colonial Problem, The, 34, 54, 56, 69, 72, 73, 77, 78, 80, 86, 101, 110.
Coupland, Professor R., 157.

Dawson, W. H., 97, 98.
De Wet, Christian, 13.
Dernburg, Bernhard, 93, 95, 171, 177.
Dove, Dr. Karl, 122.
Durham, Lord, 199.

Elgin, Lord, 199.
Epp, General von, 37, 48, 105, 212.

Erzberger, Matthias, 92.
Evans, I. L., 98.

Foch, Marshal, 20.
Fox, C. J., 198.
Fränkel, Dr., 153, 173.

George III, 197.
George, D. Lloyd, 19, 23, 24, 25, 26, 41, 96.
German Colonisation, 122.
Germany's Claim to Colonies, 34, 38, 40, 48, 85, 96, 103–5, 108.
Gladstone, W. E., 118.
Godesberg, 110.
Greaves, I. C., 69.
Grey, Sir Edward (Lord Grey), 19.

Hailey, Lord, 35, 132, 173, 182, 186, 188, 191.
Henlein, Konrad, 135.
Herodotus, 169.
Hertzog, General, 137.
Hindenburg, President A. von, 15, 16, 196.
Hitler, Adolf, 48, 69, 70, 103, 108, 110, 133, 135, 137, 206.
Hoare, Sir Samuel, 56, 114.
Hobson, J. A., 19.
Holloway, Dr. J. E., 132.
Horn, von, 91.
House, Colonel, 202.

Jameson, Sir L. S., 198.

King-Hall, Admiral, 13.
Koch, Robert, 94.
Kock, Dr. W. P. de, 124.
Krueger, Dr., 94.
Kruger, President Paul, 90, 198.
Kütz, Dr., 94.

Lansing, Robert, 38.
Leist, 91, 92, 178.

Index

Lersner, 15.
Leutwein, Major, 119, 120, 121.
Lindequist, Dr., 93.
Loymeyer, 176.
Ludendorff, General, 15, 16, 196.
Lüderitz, 118.
Lugard, Lord, 35, 101, 103, 159.

Macmillan, W. M., 98, 102.
Mair, L. P., 98, 100.
Malan, Dr., 140.
Max of Baden, Prince, 15, 16.
Millin, S. G., 166.
Milner, Lord, 22, 24, 28, 181.
Mkwawa, 146.
Monteiro, Armindo, 81.
Morel, E. D., 19.
Mukete, Fritz, 184.

Nachtigal, Dr. Gustav, 6, 88.
Neuendorf, Herr, 137.
Nicolson, Harold, 42–4, 104, 110.
Nonnenbruch, Dr., 84.

Olivier, Lord, 69.

Perham, Miss Margery, 102.
Peters, Karl, 3, 88, 89, 91, 92, 144.
Plummer, Alfred, 50, 57, 61–3.
Puttkamer, von, 91, 92, 175, 177.

Raw Materials and Colonies, 50, 59, 60, 62, 65, 267.
Roeren, 92.
Rohrbach, Dr. Paul, 121.
Rollin, M., 78.
Round Table, The, 49, 77, 133, 200.

Rudin, H. R., 175, 176, 177, 179, 240.

Said, Seyyid, Sultan of Zanzibar, 157.
Schacht, Dr., 65, 72.
Schapera, I., 102.
Schnee, Dr. Heinrich, 47, 97.
Seitz, Dr., 47, 175, 179.
Simon, M., 26, 181.
Smuts, General, 11, 26, 27, 30, 98, 166.
Solf, Dr., 93, 180.

Temperley, Prof. Harold, 15, 16, 20.
Townsend, Dr. M. E., 64, 88, 92, 94.
Trotha, General von, 91, 120, 121, 122.

Van den Heever, J., 132.
Van Zyl, Mr. Justice, 129, 132.
Vorbeck, General von Lettow, 11, 148.

Wegner, 92.
Wehlan, 91, 92.
Weigel, 135.
Wilhelm II, Kaiser, 90, 198.
Wilson, President, 15–19, 20–26, 28, 30, 37, 39, 43, 45, 201, 202, 205, 206.
Witbooi, Hendrik, 119, 120.
Woermann, 170.
Woolf, Leonard, 69.

Zanzibar, Sultan of, 144, 145, 157.
Zimmerman, A., 174, 176, 179.
Zimmermann, Emil, 115.

THE OXFORD UNIVERSITY BRITISH COMMONWEALTH GROUP

Editorial Committee

DR. C. K. ALLEN, *Warden of Rhodes House*
PROFESSOR V. T. HARLOW, *Rhodes Professor of Imperial History, University of London*
C. L. DILLWYN, *Student of Christ Church*
A. L. C. BULLOCK, *Harmsworth Senior Scholar, Merton College; Bryce Student, University of Oxford*

Senior Members

DR. C. K. ALLEN
C. L. DILLWYN
PROFESSOR V. T. HARLOW
D. L. KEIR, *Fellow of University College*
DR. J. RANKIN, *Exeter College, Controller of Lodgings*

Members of the Group who took part in the discussions

M. M. AHMAD, *India and New College*
W. D. ALLEN, *Australia and New College*
*H. F. BARTLETT, *United Kingdom and Queen's College*
G. W. G. BROWNE, *South Africa and Hertford College*
*D. BRUNTON, *United Kingdom and Wadham College*
*A. L. C. BULLOCK, *United Kingdom and Wadham College*
*C. F. BYERS, *United Kingdom and Christ Church*
A. CHRISTELOW, *United Kingdom and Queen's College*
*R. W. T. COWAN, *Australia and New College*
D. J. C. CRAWLEY, *United Kingdom and Queen's College*
G. G. CREAN, *Canada and New College*
J. L. DELISLE, *Canada and Wadham College*
*W. V. DICKINSON, *United Kingdom and University College*
*R. P. B. ERASMUS, *South Africa and Exeter College*
P. A. GIBBS, *United Kingdom and Jesus College*
*J. R. GILLESPIE, *United Kingdom and Merton College*

Oxford Univ. British Commonwealth Group

*J. E. L. GRAHAM, *Canada and Christ Church*
*DR. H. M. GLUCKMANN, *South Africa and Exeter College*
*A. G. HARVEY, *South Africa and Trinity College*
*E. P. HASLAM, *New Zealand and Balliol College*
*G. L. HOGBEN, *New Zealand and Oriel College*
G. IGNATIEFF, *Canada and New College*
C. LABRECQUE, *Canada and Pembroke College*
*H. F. LYDALL, *South Africa and New College*
J. K. MACALISTER, *Canada and New College*
M. J. C. MARKS, *United Kingdom and Christ Church*
A. D. B. MARSHALL, *Canada and Hertford College*
J. N. MATSON, *New Zealand and Oriel College*
*H. B. MAYO, *Newfoundland and New College*
*W. F. MONK, *New Zealand and Oriel College*
H. MULLER, *South Africa and University College*
L. L. MURAD, *Jamaica and Keble College*
D. J. PENWILL, *United Kingdom and St. John's College*
A. L. PIDGEON, *Canada and New College*
C. B. RAO, *India and Jesus College*
J. B. REID, *Canada and Merton College*
*G. A. RICHARDSON, *Australia and Brasenose College*
G. T. ROWE, *United Kingdom and University College*
A. C. SMITH, *Canada and Christ Church*
M. R. THWAITES, *Australia and New College*
O. H. WARWICK, *Canada and Christ Church*
E. P. WEEKS, *Canada and Wadham College*
W. WOOD, *United Kingdom and University College*

Those members whose names are marked with asterisks were responsible for the presentation of the reports which were discussed by the Group.

THE WORLD: showing British